How Our Economy Really Works

A RADICAL REAPPRAISAL

How Our Economy Really Works

A RADICAL REAPPRAISAL

Brian Hodgkinson

SHEPHEARD-WALWYN (PUBLISHERS) LTD
IN ASSOCIATION WITH
THE SCHOOL OF ECONOMIC SCIENCE, LONDON

First published in 2019 by
Shepheard-Walwyn (Publishers) Ltd
107 Parkway House, Sheen Lane,
London SW14 8LS
in association with
The School of Economic Science
11 Mandeville Place
London W1U 3AJ

www.shepheard-walwyn.co.uk
www.ethicaleconomics.org.uk

British Library Cataloguing in Publication Data
A catalogue record of this book
is available from the British Library

ISBN: 978-0-85683-529-2

Typeset by Alacrity, Chesterfield, Sandford, Somerset
Printed and bound in the United Kingdom
by 4edge Limited

iv

Contents

Acknowledgements

OVER MANY YEARS I have learnt a great deal from teachers and students of Economics, but a considerable part of this book is the outcome of informal conversations with my wife Catherine and son David over the dinner table. I am particularly grateful, however, to Dr Peter Bowman for some valuable insights. My daughter-in-law Catherine helped with several aspects of publishing. Once more I am indebted to the publisher, Anthony Werner, for his efficient and friendly services. My thanks are also extended to the School of Economic Science for enabling the book to be published.

Preface

IN ONE SENSE this book has nothing to do with Brexit.
It could have been written twenty years ago, or even much
earlier. Above all it is a response to the fundamental questions
that have confronted the UK economy for decades, and with
which successive governments of the right and the left have
failed to deal adequately. Some of these questions are obvious,
such as, 'Why does poverty still beset a large number of
people, whilst others are grossly well-off?'; 'Why are house
prices continuously rising much faster than inflation, so that
more and more people are left without a house of their own,
or are borne down by the weight of a mortgage?'; 'Why does
UK productivity remain persistently low, despite constantly
improving technology?'. Other questions are less obvious, or
are ignored through a belief in their arising from the natural
order of things, such as 'Why do the majority of workers find
themselves as employees in jobs that give them little real sense
of fulfilment?'; 'Why is there awful traffic congestion, despite
heavy expenditure on transport infrastructure?'; 'Why does
the tax system fail to bring about greater equality, despite progressive rates of tax on incomes?' All these questions, obvious
or not, are perennial ones, not particularly related to
membership of the European Union, although some extreme
advocates of Brexit might claim that they are.

In another sense this book has a lot to do with Brexit, for
the simple reason that all would agree that Brexit leaves
the UK economy in a new, unprecedented position. This
inevitably arouses both hopes and fears of substantial change.
Such hopes and fears may alike be irrational, but even so they
raise the possibility of genuine reform. Yet it is my contention

that Brexit alone does not change anything fundamental about the economy.

Why this is so emerges in the argument which follows. In short, it is that what requires fundamental reform is not any features of being or not being within the EU, but more deeply embedded ones, which have generally been established for a very long time. They are principally threefold: the taxation system, the land tenure system, and the banking system. All three are profoundly interconnected. All three require root and branch reform. The presence of concerns engendered by Brexit may provide an opportunity lacking in more equable times.

Perhaps one final concession may be made to the Brexit-eers. Fundamental reform of all three systems might be easier to carry through outside the EU. Full national sovereignty gives, at least, an opportunity to make changes to the very structure of the economy. Ideally these reforms would spread beyond the UK, or perhaps there would have been a chance of the EU itself adopting them under the influence of the UK as a member. But that would require an even greater revision of endemic ideas than reform in the UK alone would necessitate.

I

Introduction

ECONOMISTS HAVE long asserted that three factors of production lie at the root of their subject: land, labour and capital. Yet in the development of the subject into theories and practical applications there has been a thoroughgoing analysis of labour and capital and a grievous omission of the factor of land. This is reflected in the minimal place it holds in modern text books, in popular discussion and in political debate. Indeed much of the argument about major issues, like industrial production, the distribution of income and wealth and government policy, reverts to a polarised struggle between two antagonists, labour and capital. The third factor, land, hides in the background, unacknowledged yet exerting a fundamental influence upon the outcome of the whole economic process. This book hopes to present many examples of this neglected significance of land in the economy, but one obvious example may help to clarify the point initially. The price of houses has risen continuously at a rate well in excess of the rate of inflation, causing difficulties for new buyers, creating serious problems in the mortgage market, and profoundly changing the distribution of wealth between generations and between regions. Yet what is called the 'house price' is really a combination of land price and building price. These two prices operate quite differently and require quite different approaches by policy-makers. More will be said about this one example and the impact of the error upon the economy.

Why has this lacuna in economic thinking come about?

There are three reasons that have a bearing upon one another. Firstly, the land enclosure movement in Britain took place over a long period, reaching its peak in the early nineteenth century, by which time little land was left for public use and access. Private claims on land, particularly those of the major enclosing landlords, but also of all others who came to regard a piece of land as absolutely 'mine', developed vested interests. They preferred to ignore the older tradition of land as communal property to be used by individuals under conditions that took account of the interests of others. This absolute claim on land now extends to large commercial companies, including foreign ones, and crucially to the ownership of urban land, in which over fifty percent of the population now have a vested interest.

Secondly, economic thought developed on lines that seemed to justify the growth of such vested interests, whilst theoretical reasons appeared to support the omission of land from most of the analysis. It was no coincidence that as the private enclosure of land grew, alongside it grew a theory of supply and demand that only employs the concepts of labour and capital, and later a theory of macro-economics that treats the whole economy as producing and consuming in a landless environment. When land gets mentioned at all, it is usually treated as capital. The consequence of this egregious sleight of hand will be examined.

The third reason for the omission of land from economic thought is that as urbanisation developed, following land enclosure, the general awareness of the presence of land became gradually attenuated. How often do people in cities realise that they are living on land? Houses, factories, offices, shops, pavements, and indeed all the built environment, seem to establish a kind of screen between people and land. When a building is pulled down, or a road dug up, the screen is broken. Bare mud or rock provides a glimpse of the earth that lies ubiquitously but unseen beneath our feet. One result is that the term 'land' becomes associated almost exclusively with the countryside, where a minority of the population live or work. The 'land question' that so disturbed our ancestors, when it occasionally arises, is usually in the form of debates about farming tenancies or pollution of agricultural land. The city dweller is not concerned. Yet that same city dweller spends hundreds of thousands of pounds on a house, with at least half the price consisting of the land price. Similarly the worth of a retail business may be largely determined by whether it has a freehold on the land it occupies. Urbanisation makes land invisible. Only a few shrewd businessmen realise its worth, and make fortunes from trading in it.

Despite this general neglect of the factor of land, economists have usually retained a concept of land that refers not just to the dry surface of the earth, but also to the natural features attached to that surface or to the subsoil. In particular, these include natural vegetation, like forests, and minerals such as metals, coal and oil. Only when these materials are extracted by human labour are they described as wealth, production or capital. This original notion of land is a firm basis on which to examine how it operates as a factor of production. An example of this, which anticipates the following discussion of rent of land, is that the value derived from the use of land by exploiting such materials can be correctly classified as rent and not as a return on capital.

Following the founders of the subject of Economics, notably Adam Smith and David Ricardo, we may then continue to take as the starting point of any economic analysis the three concepts of land, labour and capital. Land has already been defined. Labour can be defined as the application of human effort of body and mind to the production of wealth and services, where wealth means actual physical production, excluding claims on it such as money and securities. Capital means wealth used in the production of further wealth. Retaining this threefold foundation throughout any economic discussion yields conclusions far different from the conventional ones.

2

Rent

EXCEPT IN VERY exceptional circumstances, such as plague or war, every economy produces a surplus of output over and above what is necessary to support its population. How this surplus is used depends upon the nature of the society. The surplus may be directed, for example, to cultural aims, like art or architecture, or to warfare, or to scientific development. In economic analysis this surplus takes the form of rent.

Everyone is familiar with the concept of rent. We think of it as what has to be paid to a landlord. It may be rent of a house, business premises, a farm or whatever else requires access to a site or piece of land. Such a concept, however, is too restrictive for economic analysis. The concept of rent in Economics is broader, but at the same time more precise. It may be defined as the excess value arising from a site over and above the value arising from marginal land that is only just worth occupying or using. For example, the economic rent of a piece of very fertile farm land would be the excess value of the produce over the value of the produce of a piece of land barely worth farming. This means that both values must be calculated given the same application of labour and capital i.e. the same degree of effort and skill and the same quantity of suitable capital, such as farm machinery. In the case of houses the economic rent would be the excess value of living on a particular site measured against the value of living on a site only just suitable for habitation. Value here can be considered as whatever the occupier would be prepared to pay.

A major difference between rent paid to a landlord and economic rent is that the latter is the potential rent available if the site is put to its best use. Quite often rent paid to a landlord is for an inferior use, which is allowed to continue for a variety of reasons: inertia, inadequate knowledge, sentiment or even generosity. Such reasons do not affect the economic rent. This is determined by the objective conditions operating at the site concerned and at the marginal site.

What then are these conditions that determine the economic rent? There are four main categories of these. As noted earlier, they include natural aspects of the land, like fertility, vegetation, minerals, drainage, topography and climate. Secondly there is the presence of human population. This is a critical condition, which may even make natural features of little significance. For population provides a labour force, whose quality varies considerably with education, training and character of the people, and also a market for the products of economic activity, including living accommodation. Location in a city with a skilled and active population may completely outweigh any natural features of the site, especially when these can be enhanced by man-made services, such as water supply or landscape gardening. Thirdly there is the existence of other firms in the neighbourhood, which may provide services or supplies, or may simply make the site concerned more attractive, for example for shopping or recreation. Finally there are public services, which may include transport, law and order, schools, hospitals, power and water supplies and much else which is the function of government, whether national or local. The degree of law and order greatly affects the value of a site, as do flood control and other crucial public concerns.

Given that economic rent is the potential value arising on land and not just the amount actually paid to a landlord, there are obvious questions about how this is measured. In particular there is the situation where the tenant is the landlord; in other words when the tenancy is freehold. The economic rent is clearly not zero, even though no payment is necessary. It remains what it would be were a full rent payable to a landlord.

The importance of recognising this will become clearer when an industry like retailing – to take one example – is analysed later. If a large retailer owns the freehold of a central high street site, it may appear to be making very large profits. In reality much, if not all, of these are rent. Only if this is acknowledged can the proper efficiency of firms of any type be seen. Moreover, the optimal allocation of land to its best uses can only be accomplished if the true rent is known, regardless of freehold tenure.

Economic rent can also be measured by the capital value of the site concerned. When land is sold in a free market, the price paid is approximately the capitalised value of the rent receivable in the future. This is true whatever the land use. For housing, for example, the future occupier of a house on the site pays what he or she thinks it is worth to avoid paying a rent for the site in the future; or if the house is to be built for letting the price includes the capital value of future rents to be received.

One of the consequences of the neglect of the concepts of land and rent in present-day economic thinking is that the actual differentials between the rent on different sites is often overlooked. This is partly because rent is not evident when it is not paid, as with freehold sites; and partly because vested interests are reluctant to disclose the rent receivable on valuable sites. On long established freeholds the economic rent may be hidden in the profit statements of the companies, in the private accounts of wealthy individuals, or in the beneficial occupation of land used for recreation. For example, who knows the economic rent of land held under freehold in the City or West End of London? Likewise who knows the economic rent of land held for grouse shooting or fishing in the Highlands of Scotland? Were the values of the economic rent of all sites in the UK publicly available, there might be more questions asked about whether it is being optimally used, and even about who is entitled to receive the rent.

3
Wages

A PRELIMINARY POINT about wages is that, as with rent of land, the true wages of labour may be concealed by the prevailing system of ownership. In particular, a self-employed person working in his or her own firm is really earning wages equivalent to what the firm would have to pay an employee for the services of the owner e.g. as a manager. Above this the income of the owner is profits. If his income falls below the wages level, the difference is a loss to the firm.

Britain in the twentieth century evolved into a society very heavily reliant on the Welfare State. The majority of people are mainly dependent for their living on wages which are inadequate in almost all cases to provide many of the essentials of a decent life for a family. Health services of all kinds, education for all ages, unemployment and sickness benefit, old age pensions and, for many if not all, housing require public finance on a massive scale. The term social wages has come into use to refer to this huge supplement that is needed to bring wages earned by work to a level that provides a reasonable modern standard of living.

Why is this? To some extent it is because in a democracy the majority may prefer some of these services to be provided publicly. There is a strong case, for example, for at least some health and education services to be in the public sector. Yet even so, there is no real choice about this, since the present level of wages makes proper provision for these solely out of wages impossible. Government naturally has full responsibility for defence of the realm and for law and order, but should it necessarily have to provide services that could be paid for by wage earners were wages at a considerably higher level? After all, the minority who are relatively well off often do choose private health care and independent schools.

It is a matter for public debate which services should be privately or publicly provided and, moreover, there are many different ways in which either alternative can be implemented. Politics in Britain has revolved around these questions for at least the past century. We have come to accept a fundamental division between left and right which is fostered by this issue, even if it no longer takes the basic form of capitalism versus socialism. What usually passes unnoticed is that the debate is underlain by the simple fact that wages are too low to pay for most of the services currently offered by the State.

There is, however, an even more basic aspect of the modern economy that goes unnoticed and is rarely discussed at all. Wages are too low to enable wage-earners to provide the capital required at their workplace. Owing to confusion over the meaning of the word 'capital', the situation cannot easily be recognised at all. Shares in a company are seen as its capital. So the question becomes 'Should employees own shares in the company they work for?' But the proper meaning of 'capital' in Economics is 'wealth used to produce further wealth'. Wealth is everything produced by the factors of production, namely land, labour and capital itself. Put simply, capital is the means of production, excluding land, i.e. buildings, machinery, plant, office equipment, stocks of goods and so on. Shares and bonds in firms are claims on capital – and usually on land as well – and not capital itself.

Thus the real question becomes 'Should employees in a company own the capital that they themselves use in production?' This happens straightforwardly in a business owned by a sole trader or small partnership. But usually when capital becomes substantial employees cannot afford to provide it. A carpenter may buy his own tools; workers in a modern car

factory cannot afford to buy the factory. It is now taken for
granted that, except in rare cases like the John Lewis Partnership, the firm is owned by absentee shareholders, or perhaps
by a handful of very wealthy entrepreneurs. Why is this taken
for granted? The answer is very simple: wages are too low to
enable employees to buy the very capital which they themselves use in their daily work. Were wages much higher they
might either buy capital directly or raise loans on the security
of their future income.

Current discussion of wage levels focuses on differentials.
Workers in particular industries or with particular skills
demand higher relative wages. Successful firms pay bonuses;
failing ones propose wage cuts. CEOs are criticised for earning many multiples of the average wages in their companies.
Top sportsmen and celebrities earn enormous amounts.
Women earn less than men. And so on. These clearly raise
legitimate questions. The more fundamental one, however, is
'What determines the general level of wages?' Such a general
level is difficult to quantify. Is it the average wages, the median
wage, the gross wage before deductions for tax, NIC etc., is
the social wage to be added back?

What is certain is that take-home pay is what counts for
the typical wage-earner, whether he or she is an executive in
a City firm or a bus driver. In particular, the PAYE and NIC
may just as well be seen as tax levied upon the employer of
labour. Indeed its impact on production is best analysed in
that way (see below p.32)

Why then is take-home pay so low? Total wages in the
whole economy measured in this way consistently fall well
below half of the gross national product. This means that the
majority of the population, including dependents, are receiving less in total than the share distributed in one way or
another as unearned income. Economists seem to have aban-
doned the question of what determines the distribution of
income between the three factors of production, a question
which was central to the researches of the founders of the

subject, such as the French Physiocrats, Adam Smith and David Ricardo.

The reason for this serious omission from current analysis lies once more in the development of the British economy since the land enclosure movement. With little or no land freely available, wages are inexorably forced down to the least that workers will accept. The only alternative to being unemployed seems to be taking employment at the going rate of wages. What sets that going rate? It is clearly the lowest rate at which the employer can find workers. In other words it is set by the minimum that the unemployed worker is prepared to accept. Were he or she to demand more than that, a fellow worker gets the job. The labour market – the phrase presents a useful analogy with slavery – is loaded in favour of the employer to a degree determined by the level of unemployment. Were no other workers available the employer would have to offer more, as tends to happen in particular trades in the short-run.

Yet surely there is an alternative for the worker besides being unemployed? He can become self-employed. A minority find this a genuine option, especially in industries where small entrepreneurs have opportunities, such as currently occurs with new technology. But for the great majority of workers this is not an option. How many in retailing, manufacturing, banking, transport, power, mining and construction can do this? – even if some industries, like construction, employ workers under apparent forms of self-employment.

Why is there this lack of opportunity for self-employment? There are four major reasons. The first is inability to buy or rent a suitable workplace. Workers cannot afford to pay for a site that has the right location, which is the principal determinant of the price or rent. This is true not just for individuals who could be self-employed, but even more so for those who need to work in close co-operation with others in some kind of partnership. Few groups of employees could afford to share the price or rent of a factory, office or large store.

Secondly, there is the question of capital. Employees can rarely equip themselves with the kind of capital required by modern industries. Capital includes buildings and all the manufactured articles used in a business. Very small scale enterprises may be able to purchase hand tools. A window cleaner may afford a ladder and bucket. But what of large-scale capital, like manufacturing machinery, ships or aircraft?

Even these problems of sites and capital could at least be eased for employees if credit were available on easy terms. The low level of wages makes this impossible. Banks do not offer credit on a sufficient scale for initiatives created by average wage earners. Security for credit advanced is inadequate. Banks demand security based upon assets, especially upon land. They provide short-term credit to workers only for consumer goods and long-term credit for those who can pay the deposit on a house. Otherwise their advances for productive activities are given almost exclusively to those who already possess adequate assets to provide security, in the form often of advances against land values.

The final major reason for the difficulties of self-employment is a consequence of the other three over the course of time. Most workers today do not have the inclination or ability to cast off employment and to take to the open sea of self-employment, either alone or with others. Getting a job has become a kind of social imperative. School and universities are increasingly geared to training students for some kind of employment when they leave education. The school-leaver hopes for a job in a local firm. The graduate looks to the City of London or training as an executive in a multi-national. Employment has become the deeply entrenched norm. Those who have the will and initiative to work independently are rightly regarded as exceptional and sometimes as foolhardy.

At the root of this chief feature of the modern economy lies the question of low wages. They are low because they are set by the pervasiveness of unemployment forcing them down to a minimum. But what would be the natural determinant of the wage level if unemployment were not a serious factor? The answer follows from the explanation of economic rent. The natural level of wages is the full value of what can be produced on a marginal site, where there is no economic rent. It may appear that the better sites yield higher wages. This is to ignore the proviso that work on all sites has the same degree of effort and skill, if the economic rent is to be correctly calculated. All the excess value created on better sites is rent. None is wages, except where actual differences of effort and skill are present.

Another way of looking at this is to consider an employer of labour. He or she will not pay higher wages to one employee rather than another just because the former works on a superior site. They do the same work, so he pays the going wage. A shop assistant in Oxford Street in London does not earn significantly more than a shop assistant in a provincial town. Yet the value that one produces may be well in excess of the other's. Indeed the employer might validly claim that he has to pay rent for the site that produces higher value, so why should he pay extra wages for the higher value in addition to the rent. Yet a further explanation of the relative uniformity of the wage level is that were excess wages paid on the better sites, workers would move to take advantage of them, until the wage rate was restored to the general level.

The London allowance does not invalidate this, since it merely takes account of the higher living costs in the capital city, so that real wages there are more or less at the general level for the whole country.

None of this means that differentials between wages in different occupations do not arise. They may be very large, but are caused by genuine variations in natural ability, training or character, not by the location of the work. There may also be irrational differentials regarding gender, race or age. Once more location is irrelevant. Location profoundly affects the value of the product of work on a particular site (though not usually the price of the product) but not differentials between wage levels arising from the nature of the worker. In fact, the differentials arising from location, which are economic rent, are far greater than worker differentials.

That wages are low in today's economy is not as obvious as it was in the days when children ran around without shoes and many families lacked the basic necessities of life. Poverty takes new forms, such as the necessity for two family members to earn wages in order to pay for a mortgage on a house. Nowadays the proliferation of technological devices obscures the poor quality of housing and the standardisation of cheap food and clothes. Moreover, whilst consumer goods and services have undoubtedly become more available, the relative living standard of workers compared with those with unearned wealth and income has fallen substantially. A mark of this excessive inequality is the widespread desire amongst the majority trapped by low wages to gain access to the degree of wealth of the minority by fortuitous means: gambling, speculation in paper assets, and especially by getting on to the 'housing ladder' whereby rises in land value offer benefits that in one year may even exceed annual take-home pay. Meanwhile the value placed upon work by workers themselves and their self-respect as the real producers of prosperity for their families and for society diminishes. 'Something for nothing' becomes the unspoken epigram of the economy.

4

Capital

THE AUSTRIAN ECONOMIST, Joseph Schumpeter, said that you cannot ride upon the claim to a horse. Modern economic thought and popular opinion share a similar mistake of believing that you can produce wealth with a claim to capital. All economies depend critically upon the use of capital – buildings, machinery, plant, roads, railways, ships, aeroplanes, computers and all the multifarious equipment of modern industry. Whether this is owned privately or publicly has no bearing upon this basic fact. The use of capital is one thing, its ownership quite another. Yet the belief is deeply embedded amongst all classes of society that money, shares, bonds and other financial instruments are capital. These, too, are necessary, some in the very nature of economic activity, some owing to the peculiar development of modern capitalist economies.

As a result of this gross mistake in the meaning of a word, ideas, theories and policies become not only confused but quite wrong-headed. For example, investment, which means the creation of capital goods and their innovative use, comes to mean the provision of new claims upon production. Inward investment is widely encouraged in the form of investors from abroad buying shares in UK firms. No real capital enters the country. The firm becomes foreign owned, whilst its land, labour and capital remain as British as before. Similarly UK financial institutions invest in firms abroad and capital is said to leave the country.

When investment refers to the purchase of land the error is multiplied. Land is not capital. It is not wealth used to produce further wealth, because it is not itself produced. It is a gift of nature and of the whole community. Whenever it is developed by work on improvements, such as drainage, these may be treated as capital, but in the long-run such improvements merge with the land and are best treated as part of it. When a country loses land, by ceding it to another or by sea erosion, for example, some productive power is totally lost. When capital is lost, by depreciation, obsolescence or warfare, new capital can be produced to replace it.

Drawing a clear distinction between land and capital is vital to any understanding of Economics. It follows from this that the word 'landlord' also requires a precise meaning. At present it is used indiscriminately to refer to the owner of land or buildings, or often both. The landlord is said to offer for purchase or rent a house, a factory, an apartment or an office. Yet his or her ownership of the land is logically quite distinct from the ownership of the building. Henceforth in this book the term will be used strictly as the owner of land only, just as the very word implies. The owner of a building is the owner of a capital asset, which has been produced by work and other capital. As such its owner is entitled to be paid for its sale or use. Whether the landlord is so entitled is a central issue of what follows.

The purchase of land adds nothing to the productive capacity of the economy, except in so far as it was not fully used by the seller. When derelict land comes into production a productive investment seems to have been made. But no more land has been created. The investment merely corrects the dereliction, so that the real remedy would be to avoid dereliction of useful land in the first place. On the other hand, the purchase of capital stimulates the production of capital goods. More capital is available. Work is generated both in the capital goods industries and in the industry to which the capital is applied. Nevertheless, the capital is not the finance used in the purchase. It is the actual physical goods used for production.

In the British economy today another damaging consequence follows from treating land as capital. Interest rate charges are used to influence the level of investment. When rates rise entrepreneurs are less prepared to buy new capital. This is equally true whether the finance is provided by themselves or whether it is borrowed. But the impact on the purchase of capital is quite different from the impact upon the purchase of land. This is because capital wears out or becomes obsolete relatively quickly. Entrepreneurs seek to recover the cost of the capital within its lifetime, which may be merely five or ten years. On the other hand, land lasts for ever. Hence money used to buy it is very often borrowed for longer periods, usually with a mortgage attached to the loan. Thus the interest rate has a much bigger impact on land purchases than upon capital purchases. Attempts to control the level of investment in capital by varying interest rates are largely futile. A rise in rates deters land purchases, but does little to reduce investment in capital; conversely when rates are reduced. The recent period of very low rates has not significantly helped capital creation, whilst is has had a serious effect on raising house prices, since they are largely determined by land prices. As more land is bought in response to low interest rates, the price of land rises.

Yet another mistake occurs when capital is wrongly regarded as earning a reward or income over and above its cost of production. Except in the short-run, the only factors of production that do so are land and labour, which have no cost of production but naturally receive rent and wages as their share of the output they produce. Capital appears to receive a return. If a firm invests in a new piece of equipment its income net of all other costs would normally increase. This rise is attributable to the new capital. But over the lifetime of that equipment the extra return will generally be more or less equal to its cost. Why? The reason is that if it were less the equipment would not be introduced, and if it were more the firm making the equipment – in the capital goods industry – would be able to charge more for it. In other words, new capital will receive its supply price, which is the cost of its being produced.

Of course, if there are interferences in the market for the final goods or for the capital goods, such as monopoly in either sector, the new capital may receive an extra return, called quasi-rent. This, however, is usually a short-run phenomenon, and not a feature of a normal competitive economy in the long-run.

That capital does receive a return is almost universally accepted. This error arises on one hand owing to quasi-rents, but more importantly from the more fundamental mistake of confusing capital with the finance used to purchase it. Hence capital is thought to earn interest.

Why is interest paid at all? It is the return on a money loan. The loan is often used to buy capital, so that when interest is paid by the borrower it may appear to the lender that he is receiving interest on the capital. He only really gets the interest for having lent the money. What it is used for is strictly irrelevant. If someone borrows money for a holiday, to gamble, to get married or to buy a house, interest is payable in just the same way as if he, as an entrepreneur, were buying productive machinery. This is equally true if money is lent to buy land. Interest is the return on the money loan.

The City of London, the greatest 'capital' market in the world, raises virtually no capital at all! It raises vast quantities of money loans or advances, some of which finance the purchase of capital. Who has seen machines being manufactured there? Not many are even purchased there. The City's only claim to create much capital would be when new building occurs there, in which case the actual construction, but not the land used, is capital – no doubt financed within the City.

Historically it is easy to find examples of capital formation not even involving finance provided by borrowing money. Much was built in the ancient world by slave labour. The great mansions and chateaux of the eighteenth century were financed by rents. The huge developments in Stalin's USSR, of factories, steel plants, military hardware and the rest, did not require a Stock Exchange. Capital is made from land, labour and previously created capital. Money only enters into the process as a means of exchange, and in the form of loans, if the producers do not command the financial resources needed. So, too, a modern economy, confusingly called 'capitalist', could be reformed to make money loans to finance capital investment largely unnecessary. Today, if all the claims by owners of so-called capital were cancelled, the amount of capital in the economy would remain exactly the same.

Firms naturally look for the best site that is available and affordable to set up in business, or to expand their business. They invest capital on the site by building a factory, office or shop, and equipping it adequately. One site is better than another, owing to natural factors, the urban or rural environment and the nearby public services. Thus it may appear that their capital 'earns' a better return in one place than in another. But does it? The extra return on the better site is yet another case of the economic rent of land. This is exactly analogous to the varying productivity of labour on different sites. Work in one place produces more than work in another. The workers may be identical in effort and skill, but the differential remains intractable because the sites differ. So, too, identical capital may be invested on two sites and will appear to produce different yields. The differential arises from location and not from the nature of the capital. How can identical pieces of equipment create different values of production? They could be swapped over with no change in output at either site, for the site makes the difference. That is the one crucial factor that cannot be swapped over. Every site is unique and creates a unique rent attributable to its location and qualities. This is the clearest proof that land is fundamentally different from capital, and should never be confused with it, if there is to be clarity of economic thought.

5
Structure of Industry

THE PRESENT STRUCTURE of industry in Britain is highly complex. It varies from sole traders, like local craftsmen or financial advisers, to partnerships of skilled or professional workers, like small builders, lawyers or dentists, to big companies that control many sites, like chain retailers or major manufacturers, and finally to multinationals, often foreign owned, that run vast empires of various productive units around the world.

This complexity has developed gradually. Its causes are rarely discussed. They lie in the history of how land, labour and capital have been combined and owned, but these causes still operate today, despite dramatic changes in technology and much else. Land enclosure released, or rather drove, workers from the land on which many had worked as tenants under copyhold or similar customary rights. This supply of unemployed workers moved into towns, where they became dependent on wage labour for their survival. Employers enjoyed the ability to pay the lowest wages that the unemployed would accept, so that profits rose rapidly, enabling them to expand, often from small family firms to multiple site establishments. Such profits were substantially economic rent, unrecorded as such by the freeholders receiving them. Banks gave advances for investment on the security of land and expected 'profits'.

By the nineteenth century many firms became too large for the proprietors to finance and to bear the risks on their own. The ingenious device of limited liability provided the answer. The absentee shareholder was born. Railways, cotton, wool, steel, shipping, tobacco and so on became industries run by companies financed by thousands of such shareholders, many of whom had become rich by landholding. A handful of company directors, themselves shareholders, ran each company, increasingly with independence from the views of the shareholders themselves, especially when these were content to become mere rentiers, receiving dividends paid out of profits, the derivation of which might not even interest them.

By the twentieth century the connection between ownership and actual productive activity became even more tenuous. Insurance companies and pension funds, with money raised from millions of savers, 'invested' in these ever expanding limited liability companies, in order to receive dividends and, even more, to make capital gains from growth and takeovers. Such second tier firms themselves bought land in city centres, which, while serving as office space, also enabled them to benefit greatly from the almost universal rise in land values associated with a growing population and economic development. A host of financial institutions, such as investment trusts and hedge funds, grew up like satellites.

So much has this general evolution of industry become the accepted background to the economy in Britain that it seems preposterous to most people, including employees themselves, that firms could be owned by those who work in them. Yet one only has to look at the economy from a fresh viewpoint to see through the complexities of the current structure of industry and to realise how much simpler, and above all how much more in accordance with economic justice, the situation could be.

What does an industrial town look like seen from an aeroplane? Each productive unit on the ground is a function of land, labour and capital co-operating to produce goods and services. There are no signs of shares or shareholders. One might conclude that each is a firm, or perhaps one division of a large firm, of which the people working there are the owners. Although most people today would imagine an organisation with absentee shareholders, the reality is that the productive unit itself is essentially complete with its three productive factors. The trouble is that the image of the shareholders leads to the distorted view that the whole economy consists primarily of the claims upon the productive assets of firms, rather than being the productive assets themselves. Expert commentators talk of the economic outlook improving when the Stock Exchange index rises. Investment becomes the issue or purchase of shares, rather than the creation of productive capital. The success of entrepreneurs is judged by the money they make and not by the value of their services. What Keynes called the 'money illusion' in relation to workers' tendency to measure wages merely in money values has become the general viewpoint of the population at large.

A serious consequence of most large firms being owned by shareholders is that decisions may be made by people who may have little knowledge of the firm itself, of how it operates, even of what it produces. Worse, perhaps, they may have little interest in the welfare of those who work there. This is particularly so when the owners are foreigners. They may close a plant or factory with scant regard for the unemployment created. Yet inward investment is lauded by British governments of all complexions. Such a criticism is not xenophobic. It applies equally to owners in the UK who take no interest in a company abroad beyond what they can get out of it. Absentee ownership is the real problem.

In Britain, socialism, in the Clause 4 sense of public ownership of the means of production, has long been eclipsed by the concept of a private enterprise economy. Entrepreneurs are praised, often rightly, for their ability to create wealth by their ideas and initiatives, despite being hampered by much regulation. The economy is described as competitive, an epithet that carries with it the notion of an efficient allocation of resources on the lines eloquently explained by Adam Smith. Competition in price and quality eliminates inefficient producers and elevates the efficient. Free movement of raw materials, labour and capital and access to credit are said to allow new entrants to industries and markets, so that monopoly does not inhibit the competitive model. Free access to land is discreetly made a side issue, since that might interfere with existing property rights.

Yet this last exception is the weak link in the conditions that would constitute a truly competitive economy. Consider just any two firms in a seemingly competitive market. One firm owns freehold land, the other pays rent to a landlord. They are equally efficient in their use of land, labour and capital. Is there fair competition between them? How can there be? Their so-called profits will differ by the amount of the rent paid by the second firm. In fact, the first firm in paying nothing for the land it occupies is receiving the economic rent of the site, not in money but in benefiting from the site free of charge. This is no level playing field. On the contrary, it is the seedbed of monopoly, or at least of an oligopoly of those firms with freehold land. This is clearly demonstrated in an industry like that of supermarkets. Parity of conditions creating genuine competition is only achieved if all firms in a market hold land subject to a charge commensurate with the benefit they derive from using it; which would mean that they all paid economic rent.

This almost unnoticed feature of so-called competitive markets gives rise to most of the diverse structures characterised by economists as perfect competition, imperfect competition, oligopoly and, at the limit, monopoly. Very few markets indeed can really be said to be cases of perfect competition. Those with various degrees of imperfect competition, like much retailing and small manufacturing, exhibit differences of site values and ownership that usually account for the imperfection. How many shops close down because a lease has expired and the rent has been raised? As for oligopoly, it has become the dominant form of market in Britain today. Supermarkets, oil production and marketing, mining, chemicals, banking and many more big industries are run by a small group of firms, only restrained from selling at monopoly prices by laws against cartels. Virtually all such giant oligopolistic firms own land on a large scale, making the entry of new firms exceedingly difficult.

Firms in all types of markets are greatly affected by the manner in which they have access to land. Those with freeholds have a huge competitive advantage, except in cases where they have recently borrowed large funds to buy freeholds and continue to be burdened with interest charges and repayment of loans. Inflation enhances the advantage of the freehold, which becomes increasingly valuable in money terms, whilst competitors may be paying regularly rising rents. The same advantages apply, *mutatis mutandis*, to some holders of long leases.

Rent paid to landlords drives firms' profits down to the minimum. Whenever there is rent revision, the new rent squeezes any excess profits out of the entrepreneur. Meanwhile the freeholder carries on receiving economic rent in the hidden form of 'profits'. Only if all firms were charged a full economic rent would there be a really competitive economy. Who should receive such a universal rent? Rent paid to private landlords has been the chief cause of the present structure of industry. Above all it has led to the dominant form of the limited liability company with absentee shareholders.

Were economic rent paid to the community, in the form of central or local government taxation – or even in some other way, such as the direct provision of public services by tenants of land – justice in the economic sphere would match the justice which Britain enjoys in the sphere of civil liberty. There is a close parallel. Freedom for an individual does not consist of doing whatever one likes. That, as John Locke pointed out, is properly called 'licence'. Freedom is only available if every individual acknowledges the equal rights of others. In other words freedom means free action under the law. Similarly, economic justice does not imply the right to use the gifts of nature and of the community, i.e. land, without regard to the equal rights of others. It implies the right to use land under conditions which acknowledge the rights of all others in land. This means that each tenant of land contributes to the community whatever compensates it for allowing that tenant to have unique access to his or her particular site. In short, everyone with a claim on land should pay economic rent to the community. Thus would a structure of industry emerge that exhibited an aspect of economic justice corresponding to that of our highly valued civil liberty.

What might this structure be? Partnership, which at its best follows the old rule of *uberrimae fidei* (the utmost good faith), co-operatives, employee participation in executive management: these are occasional beneficent intrusions into the common model of limited liability companies. Though they may offer promising paradigms, it may be wiser to look simply to the underlying condition that would lead to more just forms of enterprise. The essential condition is that wages rise to a level where employees can afford to own the capital that they employ in production. For then firms would use all three factors of production freely without the burden of claims by shareholders or other kinds of creditors. Where needed, credit would be provided by banks on the security of the newly found wealth of those working in a firm.

A major effect of the reform of firms in this way would be that the risk of their failing would be greatly reduced. At present most firms operate on narrow margins, unless they own the freehold of their sites. Out of revenue they need to pay wages and other costs, rent of land and taxes of many kinds: corporation tax, PAYE, NI, VAT, etc. Their profits are what remains. Unless they have freeholds, or monopoly or oligopoly power, competition reduces profits to a minimum. A relatively small fall in market demand for their products can yield losses and finally closure. Wages in particular are fairly inflexible downwards, especially where trade unions are strong, because wages are at the least that workers will accept.

Were the structure of industry reformed as outlined, wages would be flexible both upwards and downwards. Since firms would in effect consist of those who worked in them, their fortunes would rise and fall with those of the firm. Wages would be sufficient to tolerate this versatility. Indeed wages would no longer be regarded as a cost, just as shareholders' dividends are not so regarded today. Wages would be the firm's own income to be divided amongst its owners. External claims upon the revenue from shareholders and landlords would no longer be a burden. Risk would be greatly reduced.

Whatever precise structure of industry emerged, the attitude of workers would change, perhaps dramatically. Witness the difference at present between employees and the self-employed. Even in the current bureaucratic conditions of complicated rules of employment, health and safety and taxation, most owners of firms have a sense of fulfilment in their work, because they have freely chosen their trade or profession, direct it themselves and personally reap its benefits. Employees, on the other hand, work under imposed conditions. Their capacity to be creative is often stunted. Work has become primarily a question of earning a living, rather than a means to fulfilment of natural talent and energy, whilst contributing to the prosperity and well-being of the society to which they belong.

6

Property

DISCUSSION OF the rights of property is almost a
taboo subject in Britain. Any apparent criticism of
the main features draws pejorative taunts of 'Communism' or, at least, of 'Socialism'. So embedded is our
concept of property in our assumptions about society that it
is more or less excluded from any real arguments about the
economy. Existing rights of property are taken for granted as
part of the fundamental conditions which provide the framework for economic analysis and do not enter into the analysis
itself.

Yet property today is nothing but a set of rights supplemented by very occasional reference to duties. The rights
include the right to use, the right to exchange or sell, the right
to bequeath, the right to exclude others, the right to destroy
– often limited by law – and, critically, the right to receive rent.
But any questioning of the concept of property usually ignores
these individual aspects and treats property as though it were
a monolithic element in society. In fact, it does get modified
by law in marginal matters, such as the right of way given
to walkers over some private land or duties imposed in the
interests of public health and safety. These, however, do not
go to the heart of the question from an economic point of
view.

Once again the crucial distinction needs to be made
between land and other objects of ownership. Property in
buildings, man-made articles of all kinds, personal possessions
such as cars, clothes and so on may include all the above rights

without causing harm to society or to individuals. Property in land is fundamentally different.

The crucial feature that interferes seriously with the free working of the economy is the private right to receive rent for land. How is this right acquired? All property rights have their foundation in labour. What a person produces by his or her own efforts should naturally belong to that person. What right can any other individual have to it initially? Perhaps society could claim a right on the grounds that the worker would be helpless without society, but no individual could validly make such a claim.

Can land then become private property? No one produces it, for it is a gift of nature. Original property rights in land have only been claimed by force in one form or another. A history of their growth in Britain reveals this clearly, notably from the Norman Conquest to the later periods of enclosure. Once established, of course, property in land seems to acquire full rights which can be bought and sold, bequeathed and so on. In particular, the right to receive rent has become a central feature of the modern economy. When rent is accepted in this way, the land itself acquires a price measured as the capitalised value of future rents. When economists equate land with capital the circle is complete. Landed property has become a pillar, perhaps the central one, of our economy and society. Unfortunately it is a pillar that contains dry rot.

Were rent regarded as public property, the other rights in land would be modified, but not necessarily discarded. If all rent were collected as public revenue, the price of land would fall to zero, removing the market in land altogether. But security of tenure, the right to use land exclusively, would remain essential. At present we assume that this is fully upheld. This is only so for freehold landowners. What employee has security of tenure at his workplace? Some can be told to clear their desks by Monday morning. How assured of their occupancy are tenants of houses? It varies greatly depending upon the type of lease or tenancy agreement. With a mortgage the tenant is also insecure. What of the substantial minority who have nowhere to work or nowhere to live? Were absolute rights of property in land to be eliminated, security of tenure could increase greatly for very many people. A fairer system of property would be free to evolve, based upon the right of labour to receive the full reward of its efforts.

Today a worker's claim to property is disregarded in a variety of ways. Wages are the rightful property of workers, but they are held down by competition for jobs derived from a permanent pool of unemployed. They are further reduced by deductions of all kinds from the gross wages paid by employers. Charges like PAYE and NIC directly impinge upon property rights; so do other taxes like VAT. Indeed wages as the product of labour are not viewed as property at all, except perhaps when the worker is self-employed.

Claiming rights over land necessarily excludes others from exercising similar rights. Everyone excluded should be compensated for this loss of rights, if all are to be treated fairly. Rent of land is the precise measure of this compensation. If it is paid as public revenue, freedom to occupy a particular piece of land is justified by the condition that the rights of all others, or of society in general, are being acknowledged. Natural justice recognises that land is a gift of nature and not the absolute property of those who lay claim to it.

7
Taxation

THE QUESTION of taxation is generally recognised as being fundamental. What type of taxation is used greatly affects almost every aspect of the economy. Yet it is rarely seen as connected with the equally fundamental question of land tenure. In reality they are intimately connected.

What is the incidence of various forms of tax? This is not an easy question to answer, because the immediate incidence is hardly ever the final one that determines who or what ultimately bears the tax. Sales taxes, for example, appear to be borne by the purchaser of the goods concerned. If a tax, like VAT, is put on a consumer good, the price may be expected to rise by that amount, so that the purchaser pays that much more. But at a higher price fewer goods will be bought, so the seller suffers also. It may pay the seller to reduce the final price to maintain his volume of sales. How the tax is shared depends upon the relative willingness or ability to pay it of buyer and seller. This is much affected also by the degree of competition in the market.

Moreover, when the seller reduces his price and/or sells fewer goods, he will look to his suppliers and workers for a means to maintaining profits. Both of these may be forced to reduce their incomes, again to a degree dependent upon the amount of competition for their services. Some may close down or lose their jobs. Once more there are knock-on effects. The precise final impact of the initial tax rise (or fall) becomes incalculable.

Free market prices reflect the choices of consumers. When a tax is imposed the relative valuations of all goods by consumers remain the same, but the new price of the goods taxed now bears a new relationship to the price of all other goods. So consumers now make different choices. They buy less of the taxed goods and more of other goods. So their choices are distorted from the optimum pattern. This effect is increased by the fact that a price rise for any consumer good also reduces the real wages of consumers, so that their choices are once more inhibited.

What then of other taxes directly levied on wages, such as PAYE and NI? Do they simply reduce wages by the amount of the tax? It would appear so, but present wages are generally at the least that workers will accept, held down by the threat of unemployment and the minimal opportunities for self-employment. Hence employees of all degrees of skill tend in the longer-run to demand higher money wages to compensate for the tax increase. Thus the employer usually bears the tax, with similar repercussions to the impact of a sales tax. If firms raise prices as a result, this may create the threat of unemployment in their industry, so that workers do after all bear some of the effects themselves in the form of loss of jobs or of lower wages. Yet again the incidence of the tax is unpredictable.

Generally a tax on anything will reduce the amount produced. Taxes almost always deter production of goods and services, as they are an extra cost for an industry to bear. Unlike other costs, they bring no corresponding benefit to the industry. Although tax revenue may be used for public services, such as transport or law and order, there is no correlation between the tax and the benefit. The tax strikes individual firms, the benefit passes to the whole community.

What is most significant is that most taxes strike especially at the margins of production. Firstly, there is the margin in the sense of the firm operating on a marginal site. This means a site on which production with the same effort and skill as on other sites but producing less value, owing to poor location. The mining industry illustrates this clearly. Mines vary greatly in the ease or difficulty of extracting minerals. A mine on a site where the difficulty is greatest, perhaps because of the depth of the seam, or because of exceptionally resistant strata of rock, produces less per unit of input of labour and capital than other better located sites. More work and equipment is needed to produce any given value of the product. A tax on labour or capital may make such a site incapable of covering its costs and yielding a profit.

The oil industry provides a similar instance. Oil wells in the North Sea, for example, vary considerably in productivity and costs of production. A tax at the same rate on all of them would clearly penalise those on the marginal oilfields.

In retailing, work may be of an equal intensity and quality in a marginal shop when compared with one on a prime site. Yet the former produces much less value. The difference, of course, is economic rent. Taxes on labour and capital take no account of this difference, so that the marginal shops are permanently struggling, whilst their prime site competitors make fortunes if they own freeholds.

The present tax regime in the UK has gradually incorporated more and more taxes that disregard location, and tax labour and capital at the same rate on sites of different quality. Hence throughout the country marginal firms close, or depend on the willingness of their owners to tolerate minimum returns for their enterprise.

This is only one aspect of the impact of today's tax system on the margin of production. Another is even more insidious in that it is less easy to identify. Every firm employs workers up to the point, more or less, where the final worker employed just produces enough value to cover his or her wages and the costs associated with employment, such as health and safety provision. Employers may not always be aware of this natural limit to the level of employment, but it must be so. Why would they stop at employing workers who would increase their profits? Why would they employ extra workers who reduced their profits? Some firms may get this measure wrong, but their management must to some degree conform to it, if they are to survive and make profits.

What happens when uniform taxes on labour and capital are imposed? PAYE offers the clearest case. All employees pay at the same rate, subject to personal reliefs of one kind or another. Hence the marginal worker, the last to be employed, whose value just covers his cost to the employer, will immediately become a net charge on the firm and will lose his job. Thus even very productive firms on good sites will be hit by uniform taxes. On marginal sites the impact is even more harmful. Firms cannot deal with this by paying workers differential wages. The last is worthy of his hire, just like the first.

In the short-run employees may accept lower take-home pay when PAYE rises, but in the long-run gross wages must rise to maintain the wage level at the least that is accepted by workers. This occurs with any tax rise that affects all employees equally, including a rise in indirect taxes like VAT.

These two effects of uniform taxes on labour and capital, upon marginal firms and upon marginal workers, together combine to make their imposition seriously damaging to the economy. They reduce production and create unemployment. Imposed upon an economy that already restricts work to enclosed or privately owned land, and forces down wages by the existence of mass unemployment, they are devastating.

Any tax which fails to differentiate between sites of different quality is certain to affect adversely production on poorer sites more than production on better ones. It is vital to appreciate that this does not mean that less efficient firms should be taxed more lightly. Equal levels of efficiency produce unequal values of output, if the production is on sites that vary in quality. It follows that the tax level should vary with the quality of the site. Marginal firms should be more lightly taxed or not taxed at all. In other words, the tax should be based upon the economic rent of the site. This releases the marginal site from a burden that makes it impossible to meet its costs of production, including fair profits. At the same time it collects tax from the rent of sites that produce a surplus over costs arising from the superior quality of the land. Labour and capital both receive their full share in the form of wages and the supply price (i.e. cost) of capital.

A tax on rent in place of other taxes directly frees marginal or near-marginal firms from the burden of taxation. Does it similarly free firms on all sites of the tax charge on marginal workers? It must do so in that it merely collects the surplus of revenue over and above costs, including labour costs. This surplus arises from the value that the non-marginal workers produce. There is no surplus from the marginal workers and only small surpluses from the near-marginal ones. Hence there is no burden inflicted on them by the tax on rent.

Is such a radical form of taxation fair, as well as being efficient in not inhibiting production on any site which is naturally viable? One might ask why land should bear the cost of taxation, whilst labour and capital go scot-free. The answer to this moral question is very simple. It falls back upon the explanation given earlier of what are the causes of economic rent of land. Firms produce a valuable output according to the skill and efficiency of their labour and capital. They do not themselves contribute the benefits derived from their occupation of land. Land is a gift of nature. The value that it contributes arises from the four features mentioned earlier: natural qualities, population, neighbouring firms and public services, which together may be summed up as location. None of these are attributable to the firm itself. Nor are they attributable to a landlord, whether that is the firm or an external owner. The firm may decide on how to use the land, but the reward for this ability is profits, or wages if such decisions are made by employees. If the land is improved, of course, then the improvements can be regarded as capital expenditure, which should be recouped from revenue in the long run.

All four of these causes of the rent of land can be seen as contributed by the community and not by individuals or separate firms. The first comes from nature, but this is at the bidding of human settlement. The other three are direct benefits that every modern community creates. To whom then is the rent of land due? Surely to the community itself, whether its agent is central or local government or some other body acting on its behalf. For a firm or individual to lay claim to rent is to rob the community of its due. Such robbery has been perpetrated by medieval barons, modern property speculators and simply by landlords in general, whether individual or corporate. That it has become customary is no more a defence than was the outcry of slave-owners when slaves were emancipated. This in no way questions the justice of a proper charge being made for the use of buildings or other man-made property.

To call the public collection of the rent of land a tax is strictly a misnomer. If a tax is an amount levied on something that belongs to a person or firm, then treating rent as public revenue is not a tax at all. The value of land cannot in truth be owned by anyone, for no-none has a legitimate claim upon it. No individual created it. It is a gift of nature and of the whole community. So the community has the right to it.

Nevertheless, in modern conditions where land is unquestionably regarded as subject to personal ownership, the term 'tax' might be a more acceptable way of describing the public collection of the value that it yields. Justice is the rendering to each what is due to each. Land rent is due to society collectively. It is the natural fund of public revenue or taxation.

Like all principles, this one is open to the charge of being impracticable. Perhaps it is out of tune with the present widespread belief in 'my land'. But even today there is a general recognition that landowners should not be allowed to do anything they like with their land. There are laws against pollution and against cutting off water supplies, for example.

Should there not be a law against the exclusively private collection of rent?

Principles remain principles even when they are ignored. Indeed ignorance makes principles even more important. To live partially in accord with them is a great deal better than to disregard them completely. Were part of the rent collected the economy would improve. But this is subject to an important proviso, namely that there is a pro rata reduction in other forms of taxation. Without this the collection of rent would become, or at least would appear to become, yet another burden on production, although in reality it cannot itself be a burden, since it is not levied on production at all but on the unearned surplus yielded by non-marginal sites.

Were other taxes to be relieved by say 10% or 20% of the present charge, production would be stimulated, not only on marginal sites but everywhere, because taxes now bear upon marginal workers as well as upon marginal sites. Central London retailers, the best oil wells in the North Sea, fertile farms in East Anglia, but not their landlords, would all benefit, along with small out of town shops, tin mines in Cornwall and Welsh hill farmers. The relief of sales taxes, income tax, corporation tax and NIC would enable wages and profits to rise, and lead to higher employment and more investment.

Were the tax shift to go further, as it surely would once its widespread benefits were recognised, the economy could move further towards the goal of a transformation of the structure of industry. Gradually the financial ability of employees to share in the ownership of capital in their own workplace would increase. The huge fortunes accumulated from the private receipt of rent would diminish, so that the power of unearned income to dominate the economy, especially through land ownership and shareholding, would be attenuated.

At the same time the public finances would become stronger. They would be based upon the security and inherent value of the land itself, the ultimate source of all economic production, rather than upon the nefarious practice of stealing the property of workers and the providers of capital. The shape of the economy would be closer to an ideal of economic justice in which all received what is their due, including the public authorities.

8

Public Expenditure

P ARTICULARLY SINCE British governments have sought to limit budget deficits and borrowing requirements following the banking crisis of 2008, questions have abounded concerning UK public expenditure. Austerity became the order of the day, and for governments this meant cutting public expenditure wherever possible. Essential services have been pared down; non-essential ones eliminated. Such policies inevitably mean that the fiscal policy of the government, by which it seeks to influence the size of the gross domestic product by varying the level of public expenditure (or by adjusting the level of taxation) takes second place.

Clearly at the root of public expenditure problems lies the nature and volume of taxation. Although borrowing may be used to cover any deficit on the budget, there is always a limit to expenditure in the long-run set by the volume of public revenue. Governments cannot decide freely on how much to spend without reference to how much revenue they can raise. Taxation therefore remains the dominant issue. The more amply the coffers may be filled the more freedom there is to spend on public purposes.

Nevertheless, present-day public expenditure may be broadly analysed into three categories: essential, discretionary and unnecessary. Such an apportionment depends to some extent upon value judgments, but even more upon the nature of the economy itself. Essential services are those needed by every society. Firstly comes national defence against external enemies, which varies with the degree of any threat. Secondly come law and order, consisting of police and a judicial system. In recent times this has had to extend to deal with terrorist threats, and requires greater co-operation between governments and agencies abroad. Thirdly there is a range of services not easily identified, but which include flood control, waste disposal, leisure facilities and services not provided by private enterprise owing to free-riding users, such as street lighting and lighthouses for shipping.

Infrastructure, especially for transport, is another major form of necessary expenditure. In a reformed economy the transport system could be simpler, owing to changes in the distribution of population and industry (see Chapter 10 below). Whilst some transport costs are paid by users, in particular running costs of railways and the upkeep of roads by means mainly of road tax, the capital cost of infrastructure – the road system, rail track and stations – is met by public expenditure financed largely by borrowing.

Discretionary expenditure raises far more issues. This category includes education, health services, pensions, and utilities of gas, electricity and water. Public opinion has varied greatly over whether these should be provided by public expenditure or by private users of the service. At present all of them exhibit some form of both. Socialism would make most of them publicly provided. What underlies the choice, however, is the level and distribution of income and wealth. In today's economy only a small minority of people can afford to pay for education, health services and pensions out of their own incomes. Public expenditure on a large scale for these is regarded as essential by the great majority. Utilities, on the other hand, are more or less produced and sold in markets that are competitive to a limited degree, as the firms concerned are primarily oligopolies. Regulation has become the order of the day, rather than public ownership or real competition.

An economy fundamentally reformed by a tax shift would still leave all these services as discretionary, but the conditions in which choices were made would be profoundly different. Employees would have the genuine possibility of paying for education, health and pensions out of much higher incomes. Favouring public provision of all or any of these would remain an alternative, as would a hybrid system of basic public provision topped up by private fees. Excessive rivalry between socialist and 'free enterprise' options would be removed, since the distribution of income and wealth would no longer be a highly contentious issue. Unearned income would be minimised, so that differentials would be more justly dependent upon differences of skill, intelligence and effort.

Finally there are types of public expenditure that might be labelled unnecessary. What is necessary depends upon the nature of the economy. When firms, especially marginal ones, are subject to taxation based upon the labour that they employ, sales and profits, they are inevitably forced to make workers unemployed in a trade downturn or when taxes rise. A pool of unemployed becomes a permanent feature, albeit one that rises and falls. Hence unemployment benefits become a necessity, if there is to be a modicum of social justice. If, however, such a harmful tax system were abolished, the pressure on the margin of production for all firms would be eliminated. Payment of rent to a public authority would put no pressure on firms, since their ability to produce efficiently would not be impaired. Unemployment would be negligible. Only those unable to work would not be employed. For these, care should be provided with the help of public expenditure, as it is in the present Welfare State.

Much of the present expenditure, however, on relieving poverty could be reduced. Wherever poverty was caused by the malfunctioning of the economy burdened with misplaced taxes and an unjust distribution of income, economic reform would eliminate it. More relief would be available for those in genuine need through illness, injury or other disabilities. Housing benefit would disappear as houses became priced within the range of modest incomes (see Chapter 11 below).

Public expenditure as a percentage of gross national product could undoubtedly be greatly reduced in a reformed economy, where rent rather than production would be the source of public finance. At the same time, democratic choices to spend more on new or expanded social benefits might also be made.

Land value is a rich milch cow. This becomes obvious when its presence is revealed by stripping away the disguises that private interests have created for a very long time.

9

Money, Banking and Interest

MONEY IS ESSENTIALLY a means of exchange of goods and services. Without it there would need to be an extremely inconvenient system of barter. Why exchange is necessary, of course, arises from the division of labour, whereby each working person specialises in whatever they are particularly able and willing to produce. This then has to be exchanged for whatever that worker needs.

Today, however, although this basic function of money continues unabated, it has become also a medium for many other transactions which are of dubious value to the economy. In particular, it is used to trade land and labour on a huge scale.

Land is treated much like a commodity to be bought and sold with the expectation of profit. This prominent feature of modern capitalism is now so widespread that land prices far exceed those of goods and services produced by land itself, labour and capital. Land in the centre of a major city costs many millions of pounds per acre. Land on which a house is built is often worth more than the house itself. What creates these excessive land prices is the privatisation of economic rent. Were this treated entirely as public revenue, land prices would be zero. Any percentage of rent taken as public revenue would give a proportionately lower land price.

Labour, too, is assumed to be a kind of marketable commodity, not totally unlike slaves once were. We talk of a labour market and of human resources. This is an infringement of human dignity. Employed workers are paid wages at the going rate in the so-called market, but at root this is no more than a means of returning to the worker merely a share of the value which he or she has produced. Were most workers self-employed this would be obvious: what they received would be part of the net revenue of the firm.

Land prices, particularly those that make up a substantial proportion of 'house' prices, have now risen in Britain to a point where they seem to deflate the value of actual work and production. Many householders find that their house (and land) price rises by more in one year than they have earned in that year. What is a wage rate of say £25 per hour when compared with a 'house' price of say £300,000? One serious effect of this discrepancy is that many of those without houses – usually the younger generation – find it impossible to buy one. Instead they rent at a rate in step with the price of the property of which they are tenants.

Another example of the deleterious devaluing of money, not itself directly related to land values, occurs in the foreign exchange markets. Well over 90% of the money that changes hands in currency transactions is not being exchanged to finance international trade or investment. It is mainly for speculation in currencies, related to future expectations of short term developments, including those of international interest rates. Speculation, except on a minor scale that helps to stabilise a market, further diminishes the function of money as a means of paying labour and capital and facilitating trade in goods and services. Few questions are asked about the source of large quantities of money being used merely for speculation.

In almost all such cases of money used and misused, the type of money is not notes and coins, which are the small change of the monetary system today, but bank debt. This provides for all substantial transactions of production and trade, and for purchases of land, houses, shares and foreign exchange alike. Bank credit and debit cards also convert many personal transactions from cash to bank debt.

So what is bank debt? Everyone regards the money in their

bank account as part of their personal wealth. Yet curiously few people ask where such money comes from! It certainly does not come from deposits of notes and coins at banks. Yet even many bankers seem to believe that its source is the deposits that are made by bank customers.

Deposits at a bank arise mainly from transfers of funds from another bank, which follows when a payment is made into someone's account by cheque, credit card or debit card. For this reason all individual banks appear to be receiving deposits, which bank clients can use to pay their own debts, thereby transferring deposits to another bank. But if one looks at banks collectively it is clear that this does not explain at all how the deposits arise in the first place.

The answer is simple. They come from bank advances. As the old textbook adage correctly insisted, 'Every advance creates a deposit'. 'Creates' is the operative word. Banks create money. By giving an advance they grant a customer the right to draw cheques (or cash) up to the limit of the advance. The customer makes out the cheque in payment to a creditor, who pays it in as a deposit at a bank. Hence the latter bank is indebted to the depositor, whilst the former bank is a creditor to the customer who accepted the advance. The new deposit is money that did not exist before the advance was granted. The first bank has created this new money. So the whole process begins with the advance, not with the deposit. Individual banks may relate their capacity to give advances to their current rate of receiving deposits, but in the whole system advances equal deposits. Successful banks may receive more deposits than others and be encouraged to extend their advances. In this sense banks may be said to compete for deposits and thus appear to be re-lending to new customers. Thus the false belief arises that the deposits are the source of bank money, a belief not far removed from seeing money as manna from heaven.

Since banks create money they are crucial elements in the economy. Only a limited number of financial firms can be allowed to qualify as banks in view of this significance, although there could be enough for them to be competitive. At present there is an oligopoly of a few large institutions, enabling them to dominate their customers.

This tendency to concentration has been assisted by the present deregulation of the banking system. One highly damaging result has been the proliferation of fraud and a dangerous mushrooming of advances given without due care to their viability.

There is a natural limit on who can become a banker. It has to be a firm which is trusted by people in general and, in turn, knows how to trust people in particular. Anyone can give credit or lend money to others, if there is mutual trust, but only a few institutions are trusted throughout the whole economy. No one takes a cheque drawn on an unknown banker. Equally, judging the credit-worthiness of someone seeking an advance requires special skill and training. Local banks might operate within geographical limits determined by the extent of their trustworthy reputation.

A wise economist said that bankers are the ephors of the exchange economy. Ephors were the five senior magistrates in ancient Sparta. In a modern economy bankers are the judges of which business enterprises can open and expand by receiving advances with which to finance their capital and productive activity. Capital projects need time to yield revenue and profits. Meanwhile the employment of both capital and labour needs credit. Stock and capital assets must be bought and used, and workers employed and paid wages, in advance of the sale of the product, especially if the product itself is a capital good, such as industrial machinery. Trade credit helps with this process, but bank credit in the form of advances is the key element.

In the British economy today this vital function of banks is hindered by other activities to which they are diverted. Most notably banks are drawn into giving advances for the purchase of land. On the one hand there is land used as productive sites – for factories, shops, warehouses and so on. The excessive price of land means that bank finance is needed for the so-called investment in land. On the other hand advances are given on a huge scale for the purchase of land for housing. This is not merely land for new housing projects; it also includes all the land bought when existing houses change ownership.

Moreover, bank advances are rarely given now without collateral security given by the borrower. This very often takes the form of land; hence banks favour large landowning firms and make small businesses struggle to obtain credit.

Land purchases do nothing to finance production, since land is not produced. They simply raise the price of land, making it even more difficult for firms to obtain it for production and for individuals to buy houses. Indebtedness to banks rises to enormous proportions, mainly in the form of mortgages that may take decades to repay. Until the 1980s building societies provided loans for house purchase. These were financed by the societies' deposits from investors. By this means no money was created. When most of the societies were allowed to change to become banks, they also started to give advances and thus create deposits. House prices rose even faster as a result, so that they now are at levels of many multiples of the average income of would-be house buyers. This undoubtedly contributed to the banking crisis of 2008, and could easily contribute to another one.

Banks have also been diverted from their real function of financing production by their excursion into giving advances for the purchase of consumption goods. Mainly this is in the form of credit cards. This also does little to help productive activity, except in so far as it enables consumers to purchase consumption goods in advance of their earning the requisite wages. Such bank credit must be inflationary, unless repayments of card credit keeps pace with sums advanced. An economy that relies on bank credit to finance consumption expenditure is building on shaky foundations.

In modern conditions, which have developed from the unscrupulous eviction of the mass of the population from the land that is their collective inheritance, bank advances for the purchase of land have become a necessity. Without them businesses and house owners would fail to obtain access to land. Only by a tax shift that makes rent into public revenue can land prices be substantially reduced to make land more available for productive and domestic use. Thereby bank credit would be released for its proper function of financing industry.

Even were bankers to realise that their advances should be directed at productive enterprises and not at land purchases, they would nevertheless be unable on their own initiative to improve matters a great deal. For the root cause of the whole problem is the privatisation of land values. If this remains, bank finance to purchase them inevitably follows, as firms and individuals must have access to land.

With zero land values, commercial property and houses would be very considerably cheaper. Property prices would be based upon building costs – labour, materials, architects' fees and so on. Bank advances would still be necessary to finance these, but they could be repaid over a moderately short period. Whereas rising land prices are a major cause of inflation, as money is created without any corresponding output, advances for buildings only create money which is matched by the value of the buildings produced. Advances for pre-existing buildings would only be slightly inflationary, provided that they were repaid within any particular period.

The question of interest rates remains to be examined. Like private land values, interest payments have become a cardinal feature of capitalist economies. Indeed they almost define what capitalism has become. The widespread belief is that interest is paid for the use of capital. This goes back to the original misnomer. Capital is wealth used for the production of further wealth, where wealth means anything useful that is produced. Money, or claims on wealth such as shares, are not capital. When capital goods are produced their price covers the cost of production, including a fair profit for the producing firm. No extra payment is required or appropriate. Any premium paid indicates some degree of monopoly in that particular capital goods industry. Such a monopoly element in profits is in no way an interest payment.

But, the argument runs, surely the firm investing in the capital, i.e. using it productively, should receive interest as a return on the investment? There is no good reason why it should. If the industry is competitive the firm should only receive a return to cover its costs, including the cost of the capital and normal profits.

Why is it assumed that capital receives a return called interest? The explanation for this error is that interest is really a charge made for a money loan. Loans are often required in order to defray the cost of capital, especially on large projects, such as buildings, transport assets or other infrastructure. Here the interest charge on the loan is mistakenly seen as a payment for the use of the capital itself. Confusion is confounded by regarding the productive capital and the loan as both being capital.

Should banks then charge interest on advances? It is assumed that they are justified in doing so; but there is a critical difference between an advance and a loan. The latter is the lending of existing money by a lender to a borrower. Since the lender is depriving himself of the use of the money for a specific time, he is perhaps entitled to ask for an amount in addition to the repayment of the loan itself. Moreover, the lender is running the risk of default in repayment. Hence the interest charged may vary with the risk involved. For his part the borrower is paying for the advantage of obtaining immediate use of funds that he does not possess.

Banks, on the other hand, do not make loans in the course of giving advances. They do not have the money that they advance; they create it. This is done, as it were, by the stroke of a pen or the impulse of a computer. The labour involved is minimal, although there is skill and judgment in assessing the creditworthiness of the customer. The full costs of providing the service of giving an advance — the cost of premises, administration, accounting etc. — need to be compensated, with a small addition for the risk that the customer may default, which would probably leave the bank with debts outstanding to other banks. But the bank, unlike the lender of a loan, is not denying itself of the use of funds. The customer is simply paying a fair price for the service.

There are three main reasons why banks today are able to charge interest on advances. Firstly, industry is no longer financed by those who work in the industry. Firms desperately need outside finance, some of which can only be provided by banks. Secondly, advances in the form of mortgages on house purchases have become far greater with the enormous rise in land prices that are disguised in the price of houses. Thirdly, banking is no longer a competitive industry. It is dominated by a handful of large banks that form an oligopoly. They do not therefore compete sufficiently to bring the interest rate on advances down to zero. For these three reasons banks now hold the economy to ransom for so-called interest charges, especially on house mortgages.

The present system of banking in Britain encourages the practice of speculation in land values. In a growing economy, or even in one that simply suffers from inflation, land speculators can make vast 'profits' from buying land and holding it out of use whilst its price rises. The forfeit of rent meanwhile is more than compensated by the rise in the land price. This speculation is often hidden in the complicated business deals in which firms holding land are bought and sold. Under the heading of 'goodwill', for example, a firm with a valuable site is sold with a large 'profit' which is really increased land value. Similarly, farm land is bought, which when granted planning permission, rises greatly in value. Banks give advances for such speculative ventures. If they charge interest on the advance, the speculator can usually afford it. It seems that the interest is a legitimate return to the bank out of a capital gain that it facilitates. In reality there is no capital involved, only the creation of money to purchase an appreciating asset.

Likewise the provision of advances to finance mortgages offers similar opportunities for house owners to make large gains from the land element in the house price. Banks connive in this by offering advances secured on the value of the house – with its land. Indeed very many commercial bank advances are on the security of land also.

For genuine loans an interest charge is a fair transaction. Money needs to circulate for capital projects of all kinds. Banks alone need not provide all the finance required. Today's economy, however, grossly exaggerates the need for both loans and advances, owing to the extreme mal-distribution of wealth and income. Industry now depends upon the sale of shares to those with available funds. Without interest payments, usually in the form of dividends, such funds would not be forthcoming. But this mal-distribution is a consequence of the existing system of land tenure and taxation. It is to these that economic reform should direct its attention. The reform of banking would follow naturally.

10

Transport

NO ASPECT of the economy more obviously involves location than transport, since it is concerned entirely with the movement of people, goods and capital from one location to another. The effect of transport systems upon the location of population and industry is profound, yet in many respects the effect is disregarded. Probably the first question asked by the founder of a business is where to locate it; and the answer is largely influenced by the transport facilities available for workers, supplies, final goods and consumers. Present-day firms are more likely to locate where there is quick and ready access for skilled labour and consumer markets, rather than for the supply of raw materials which are no longer so much bulky loads, like coal and iron ore. Moreover, as transport technology develops the choice of location varies accordingly.

Other technological developments, especially in communications, affect the location chosen. Computers, mobile phones and other technology make it possible for workers and firms to locate far from what would have been regarded as their obvious place of work. Yet this does not seem to have changed radically the concentration of firms and working populations in towns and cities. Physical proximity remains a major factor in location for a range of reasons: personal relationships, including the trust arising in direct human contact; external economies of all kinds, i.e. economies that arise not just within a firm but owing to the presence of others; availability of public utilities like power, water and law and order. Urban transport systems also play a key part in maintaining the attraction of concentrated economic activity.

A central question regarding the economics of transport is how it is financed. Few transport systems, if any, can be fully financed out of fares and freight charges. If these alone are the revenue, there has to be a subsidy from national or local government. This strongly suggests that there is a serious oversight in the economic thinking involved.

The oversight can be stated in one sentence. Transport systems benefit, not just the users, but also localities. A road benefits all who live or work near it. So, too, do railways, waterways, ports and airports. Contrarily, those who are located far from transport facilities are handicapped, unless they seek a quiet, and probably leisurely, life. The network of transport links on a map is a clear indication of the locations of more or less intensive areas of economic activity.

Under the present system of land tenure, those individuals or firms who own land with good transport facilities benefit without any corresponding payment for the services, except where local authorities subsidise these out of the council tax. Such landowners are free riders. They gain twice over; once as users of the services (for which they pay, like all other users) and secondly in the higher rents or sale prices that they can obtain for their land, for which they pay nothing. No surprise that transport cannot be adequately financed by user charges alone!

Public collection of the rent of land would meet the demands of finance and of natural justice. All beneficiaries would share the transport costs more or less proportionately to their benefits. Subsidies then paid to transport operators could be directly related to the value created by particular services.

Transport systems require very heavy capital expenditure on infrastructure of all kinds: roads, rail-track, bridges, tunnels, signalling, port facilities, airport runways, administrative buildings etc. It is the existence of this infrastructure that gives rise to the enhanced value of locations that benefit from them. Hence a charge on land values could be used to finance these capital costs, whilst running costs, including capital maintenance, could be met by those who incur them directly, namely the users. Capital costs are clearly what make the overall financing by fares and freight charges alone impractical.

Nevertheless, the provision of finance in this way would need to be adapted appropriately for particular transport systems. For example, should road users pay charges in the form of tolls or road taxes? Should rail users pay according to the distance travelled or in some other way? How much of the rent collected from landowners should be used for transport purposes, since it arises from more than the existence of transport facilities? Can user charges be efficiently and accurately collected?

Ports are an interesting case that raises further questions. They demonstrate clearly how any transport system is a natural monopoly. As with roads and railways, no two ports would be economic if built adjacent to one another. Moreover, a port has a hinterland that requires importing and exporting services and facilities for passengers. But a single port has the power to charge monopoly prices. Accordingly ports should not operate as though they are firms in a competitive market, although they do face limited competition from other forms of transport. Public control should moderate the natural monopoly power, either by full public ownership, preferably local, or by regulation.

The same argument applies to airports. Their hinterlands may be less clearly demarcated, but public rent collection nationwide would make this irrelevant. It would be left to national and local government to decide how best to allocate capital expenditure on airports, at the same time as regulating the prices charged to users.

A feature which distinguishes airports from seaports is the elaborate retailing facilities, where tax free goods are available. Major retail chains, especially, take advantage of the concentration of international passengers to find lucrative markets. When airports are privately owned the economic rent from these markets is lost to the public purse, despite being created by the presence of air transport routes and captive customers. Managing an airport earns a fair reward, but the locational advantages for retailing arise from the clustering of shops, available labour and the presence of public services, particularly rail and bus connections.

Aircraft take-off and landing slots offer further legitimate opportunities for public rent collection. Competition for these, which are necessarily strictly limited in number, makes them very expensive. They have a monopoly price of their own. Their value is derived largely from the location of the airport near a major conurbation, or from its status as an international hub. Private interests have no rational grounds for benefiting from this peculiar value. Private enterprise is rightly rewarded for its efforts in building and perhaps managing an airport, but why should it gain from the premium received for scarce location in space and time?

Transport systems are naturally self-financing to a large degree. They create wealth in the areas they serve by their very presence. Their running costs may be fairly met by users, but their existence costs should be met from the extra wealth that is generated in the form of land rents. This applies both to the land occupied by the transport facilities and to the land that benefits from their presence. If the system is publicly owned, of course, the rent of the site would fall naturally into the hands of the public body concerned.

The British economy suffers seriously from a lack of adequate transport services. Roads are blocked by huge traffic jams; railways are grossly overcrowded in rush hours, particularly in urban areas. Rapid transport systems in conurbations seem unaffordable. New ports and airports meet vehement local opposition. Modern technology might be able to deal with some problems, if adequately financed. At present much expenditure on transport goes to landowners when their land is required. This is recorded as part of the capital cost, even though no capital is created by it. Such 'capital' expenditure is paid out perhaps before a single ton of concrete has been laid down. If land was treated as a public asset, it could be obtained merely by a payment to compensate the occupier for disruption.

Were rent of land to be available for the finance of transport systems, new transport developments of all kinds would create wealth, not just in areas like south-east England, but throughout the country. This is not only a financial matter. Transport is necessarily a function of the geographical distribution of population. Massive urbanisation, which continues to this day, originated in the great land enclosure movements of the Tudor period and the late eighteenth and early nineteenth centuries. Enclosure of land was not all of a kind; some was for genuinely economic reasons, to consolidate agricultural land in the hands of farmers introducing new methods and equipment. Some, however, was merely carried through by landlords seeking to gain from the rising price of land as economic development demanded fresh sites. Other landlords held land out of use whilst its price rise outstripped the profits to be made by immediate use. In many areas traditional small farmers and labourers suffered greatly from the loss of their ancient and often undocumented rights over land. In towns and cities many more suffered from the appalling conditions of some factories and housing.

All this led to excessive urbanisation as an outcome of the Agrarian and Industrial Revolutions. The prime cause was ignoring the rights of the whole community in land. In particular, the duty of those holding land to pay rent to the community was neglected. Modern transport systems have been built to cater for the prevalent concentrations of population. This acerbated the situation: canals connected industrial areas; railways and roads ran between larger towns and cities; London became the hub of the railways and continued to focus new trunk roads and then motorways.

Today we see huge fleets of lorries and vans exceeding the railways in carrying food, raw materials and manufactured goods according to the pattern of this geographical development. Cars are ever more concentrated in urban areas, causing enormous delays and frustration. Yet in rural parts there is a dearth of public transport, with local railways reduced widely after the Beeching cuts of the 1960s, and local bus routes closed down or reduced. The whole transport system reflects a deep imbalance in the distribution of population.

Both public opinion and transport policymakers ignore the underlying cause. There is a clamour to improve rail and road services, with little or no regard to the question of why such extensive development is needed. Why are goods transported hundreds of miles to factories or markets? Why do millions commute large distances to work? The answer is too simple to be noticed: people and production are artificially spaced out, heavily in urban concentrations and sparsely in rural areas.

What has the rent of land to do with all this? Were rent collected as public revenue, rent-seeking entrepreneurship would cease. Firms would not be so strongly attracted to areas of high rent, such as central London. Land would not be held out of use. Marginal enterprises, both agricultural and industrial, especially in rural areas, would revive. Huge firms would not control national markets, with the attendant need to transport goods from enormous warehouses to distant retail outlets. A balanced distribution of population would offer more spacious, healthier and fruitful lives to people long constricted by an enclosure of land more virulent than when the first smallholdings were taken over by greedy landlords.

II

Housing

ECONOMIC THINKING about housing is grossly distorted by one fundamental oversight. The price of a house in reality consists of two quite different prices: the price of the land on which the house is built, and the price of the building itself. These prices are determined in completely different ways, and affect the final composite 'house' price very differently. Land is not produced. No more of it can be made and, even though land use can be changed so that land can be transferred to housing from other uses, the total supply remains the same. Moreover, the location of every house site is unique. On the other hand, the price of a building is subject to the usual laws of supply and demand. If price rises, more labour and capital can be brought into the building industry. If they fall, these can move into other industries. Thus the supply of buildings is intrinsically elastic; it responds to price changes. This happens more in the long-run, of course, but that is of minor significance when compared with the impact of the fixed supply of land.

Housing land prices are above all determined by location. Other factors, like topography, drainage, flood risk and climate are influential, but the precise location is the dominant factor. A house in the West End of London may be worth many multiples of an identical house in a northern town. A house on the south coast of Devon may be many times the price of a similar one on the north-west coast of Scotland. Yet the building costs of each of these two instances may be nearly the same. Nowadays such locational features as proximity to good schools or new transport links have become important.

The implications of this basic distinction between land price and building price are extremely far reaching. In particular, it accounts for the excessively high price of housing generally. High land prices, causing high house prices, have a great range of harmful effects.

Firstly, over the years they have produced three kinds of unfair differentials. Most obvious are the differentials between rich and poor. Those who have owned houses for many years have become relatively rich. House prices have risen much faster than the inflation rate. Those without houses have been left behind; they are the new proletariat. The argument that a high house price is not really a great advantage, because if one moves house one faces a similarly high price is facile. House owners do not have to pay rent for housing. Also they can raise money on equity financing. They can spend their income with little need to save, since the rise in house price does the saving for them. For many people their wealth now lies largely in their house value. Their children benefit if they inherit the house. Since land prices arise from benefits conferred by nature and by the community, these wealth differentials are an entirely gratuitous gain for the house owner, unrelated to rational differences, like productive effort or skill.

Another form of unfair differentials is the generational nature of the wealth created. Older generations have a much greater share in land values, because they have bought houses and often paid off mortgages. Year by year it becomes more difficult for younger people to buy houses, owing to the grossly inflated price of the land on which they are built. Older people have become relatively rich by the mere process of inhabiting a house for a number of years. An indication of this is given by the increase in the ratio between average incomes and house prices, reflected in the fact that mortgages were once limited to two or three times gross income and now stand at perhaps eight or ten. A young couple embarking on home ownership can look forward to mortgage repayments for almost a lifetime. Moreover, it is usually both incomes of a couple that must bear the repayments. As a result, women, in particular, no longer have a free choice as to whether to go out to work or to stay at home with children. Yet political correctness now claims that women have more choice. Their new-found 'freedom' often consists in having to work in order to pay the mortgage.

There is a third form of a differential caused by high land prices that underlie house prices. Regional variations are very considerable, especially between south-east England and the rest. In very general terms, the north, Scotland and Wales lag some way behind. This has several harmful effects, in addition to those already discussed. Mobility of labour is reduced. To move from an industrial northern town to London becomes almost impossible for those who wish to buy a house. Equally a move in the other direction, whilst it may offer a superior house, is probably a one way change of location. This immobility is damaging to the economy, as it inhibits the flexibility that an entrepreneurial system demands.

A particular feature of this immobility is the problem of inner city accommodation for those on low incomes. This is especially acute in the case of vital public sector workers, like nurses, social workers, bus drivers and other lower-paid workers. This problem notably affects smaller cities and not just large conurbations. Regional variations of house price are also a general limitation on people's freedom of choice as to where to live, regardless of economic considerations.

The disparity between high land prices and the price of the buildings also makes for poor quality housing. Developers look to easy money from the land rather than to profits from good quality buildings, especially as the latter are determined competitively. The result is inadequate space, poor design and cheap materials. Buyers are spending much more on the location of the house than on its quality as a building.

As land prices rise, rents of accommodation rise accordingly, for they are a reflection of property prices. Thus the alternative to buying a house, namely to rent a house or apartment, becomes increasingly expensive. Buying to let has become a major form of so-called investment, reinforcing the landlordism that is an endemic cause of economic problems. Government action to restrict rents simply reduces the supply of rented property, which also pushes up house prices yet further. Government financial assistance with rents or housing benefits becomes a heavy charge on the Exchequer, and serves also to put more money in the hands of landlords. Every way one turns, the presence of private land values undermines a fair and efficient housing system.

House prices today are intimately related to the provision of bank credit. This is an inevitable consequence of high house prices and low wages. Since interest payments on mortgages are similarly established, there are wide repercussions for financial markets. A damaging feature of this interdependency of housing and interest charges is seen in Government monetary policy. Interest rates have become a prime tool by which the economy is directed by the Bank of England. Indeed fiscal and other policies have largely given way to the use of variable interest rates. The level of investment and consumer spending are regarded as amenable to interest rate changes. Yet this manipulation of interest rates has quite different impacts on different sectors of the economy. In particular, rates on mortgages affect the volume of bank credit taken up by the housing sector, whilst those on credit directed to industry influence the volume of new investment in productive capital. Hence when the Bank of England judges that it is timely to change rates for the housing market – to raise them because banks' financial security is threatened by excessive mortgage advances, for example – this ineluctably impinges upon new industrial investment. The latter intervention may be quite untimely. As a means of control over the economy interest rates have become a blunt weapon at the least and a dangerously random one at the worst.

The link between bank mortgages and house prices has yet another potentially disastrous effect, as was witnessed in 2008 with the banking crisis. Banks may misjudge the extent to which rising house prices (caused by escalating land prices) may go beyond a sustainable level. A rapid price fall as house buyers leave the market sends those with very high mortgages into negative equity, as the outstanding debt exceeds the house price. Owners may default on repayments and cannot sell without becoming insolvent. Sub-prime mortgages, when the initial security of employment and income is inadequate, greatly accentuate the problem. The banks may make poor judgments of credit-worthiness or take unjustifiable risks. Once more the real cause of this situation is the land value element in the 'house' price. Without it a purchaser would need only to finance the price of the building. Mortgages would be greatly reduced and would be secured against bricks and mortar rather than against volatile land prices.

What is required to solve the perennial housing conundrum is the acceptance in the community that land values are contributed by nature, society and public services; that private claims upon them are at root unjustifiable. This would be a major change of heart on the part of the ordinary house owner. But the sacrifice, if seen as such, could be made gradually. A land value tax, rising step by step from a low level, would slowly bring down 'house' prices. As they fell, the ability to buy and sell houses would be improved. Those wishing to move house would obtain less when they sell, but pay less when they buy. First time buyers would enter the market more easily. Only perhaps those who buy houses as an investment would find themselves worse off. Would this be such a disaster? Should peoples' homes be a proper object of speculation and a proper source of unearned income? Those whose business is to finance the purchase of buildings, as opposed to land, would continue to make a living. The housing market and house prices would become truly what the terms imply.

12

Public Utilities

PUBLIC UTILITIES, such as water, gas, electricity and communications, are in certain respects natural monopolies. In this regard they closely resemble transport systems and similarly require careful analysis into what degree of monopoly power is naturally inherent in them. To take one obvious example, the national electricity grid system is clearly a unitary mechanism extending over the whole of the UK, for which competing systems would be ludicrous. Yet the actual supplying of electricity to homes and businesses may have a competitive element.

For this reason there is inevitably much debate, often political in nature, over the question of whether ownership should be in private or public hands. Competitive capitalism and socialism have polarised the arguments. Neither can completely deny the presence of both natural monopoly and competitive aspects. As a result the UK has seen successive waves of nationalisation, privatisation and the half-way house of public regulation. These views each have their validity, and reflect the opinions which in a democracy have legitimate outlets and means of implementation.

However, although the debate in Britain mainly takes the form of public versus private ownership, there are other possibilities, such as state-owned companies or non-profit making corporations independent of government.

A more technical version of the question finds that, owing to great economies of scale, these industries have costs per unit of output that fall as greater quantities are produced.

Once very large capital installations, like reservoirs, pipe-lines or telephone masts, are installed, the unit cost falls very low. But the market for the output has an upper limit. Even free services would not have an unlimited demand. Hence the whole market can most economically be met by a single producer. More than one would mean higher unit costs. This confirms the commonsense view that duplication of very large capital projects is uneconomic. So the problem of who should own, or control, the monopoly service remains open.

Unfortunately this easily becomes the conclusion to the debate as an economic issue. The question of the part played by land is once more left to one side. Yet utilities are deeply embedded in land, literally and metaphorically. Reservoirs occupy huge areas of land, and provide the element of water, which in its natural state as rain and rivers is included in the economic definition of land. Pipe lines criss-cross land, usually beneath the surface. Electricity and telephone pylons, windmills and other utility installations are erected on fairly extensive sites.

How does such land enter into the provision of the service concerned? In the UK it is bought or rented from private owners. The price of the land, or its rent, enters into the cost of the service, so the utility user ultimately pays, except to the extent of any public subsidy paid by the taxpayer.

What have landowners contributed that justifies what they receive from users or tax-payers when planning permission is granted for a public utility on their land? If they improve the land to make it suitable for installing capital, clearly they should be compensated, but natural qualities, like topography, climate, soil and, above all, location, are in no way the result of any effort or skill of landowners. Why should they be paid for providing these? Is the payment in reality a bribe to induce them not to withhold the land from use? There must be proper regard, of course, for security of tenure, so that land is not taken arbitrarily from rightful tenants. But the law should distinguish between such rights and the unfounded right to sell or receive rent as an owner.

If rent of land were collected as public revenue, the issue of private or public ownership of utilities would be simplified. If a utility were privately owned, then it would pay land value tax, with the land being valued in its present use. If it were publicly owned, the tax could be waived. In no case would the tax be passed on to users of the utility, as this would mean the utility was exploiting its monopoly position. Regulation might be needed to prevent this happening, because normally it is competition that prevents a land value tax being passed on.

The inclusion of the value and ownership of land in questions about investment in utilities and about the consumer prices of their products would yield a clearer picture of their real costs and benefits to the economy. Public or private ownership and regulation would receive more rational consideration.

A further issue remains, which has its counterpart in relation to transport systems. Utilities create very substantial external economies and sometimes diseconomies. When a new supply of water, gas, electricity or telecommunications is installed, there are clearly benefits, and often some harm, associated with it. How are the beneficiaries, or losers, to be charged or compensated? The users of the service pay bills, but others are affected also. In areas near or closely connected with the new supply land values rise. Once more it is not the landowners who create this extra value. Equity demands that they pay the extra value that they receive to the public purse by means of a revaluation of the land for tax purposes. Likewise any damage or inconvenience caused by a new installation should attract a reduction in land value assessment. Such treatment is analogous to that suitable for transport systems.

Public policy on utilities could similarly follow the transport model for pricing. Consumers would pay the operating costs, incurred by the use of the service, whilst the Exchequer would pay the fixed charges, or existence costs, from land tax revenue. If the utility were privately owned, it should receive a subsidy towards the capital costs, i.e. the fixed charges.

A final point concerns technology. Technological advances are now rapid and far-reaching. In telecommunications particularly they have greatly changed the form of communications in the private, business and public spheres. As a consequence, the distinction between existence and user costs may itself vary, and even become obscure. Services that were naturally monopolistic, like land-line telephones, become available on a competitive basis with mobile phones, for example. The distribution, as opposed to the generation, of power supplies similarly has undergone radical change. Yet such developments in no way need undermine the fundamental distinction between the use of natural resources, which include the electro-magnetic spectrums, for example, and the use of the services provided by labour and capital. The latter factors earn the reward of wages and the supply price (cost) of capital; the natural resources receive rent, which should be collected by such means as a land value tax. For natural resources to an economist are land. This distinction should be acknowledged by society, or ignored at its peril.

13
Retailing

WOULD NAPOLEON today call the British a nation of shopkeepers? If so, he would surely have to refer in some way to the dominance of retail chains and supermarkets. No longer are there millions of self-employed retailers running family shops in every city, town and village. The nation of shopkeepers has become a nation of chain store employees.

Whilst small retail firms are everywhere in Britain under pressure from these giant chains, like Tesco, Marks and Spencer, Arcadia Group or Costa Coffee, few people notice a vital underlying condition that is largely responsible for this historical and accelerating transformation of retailing. In retailing markets the method of land-holding largely determines the outcome. Shops are controlled, not by entrepreneurs alone, be they small or large, but by entrepreneurs and landlords. These may be the same, i.e. the entrepreneur owns the freehold or a long lease, but to distinguish between the two functions is – as always – crucial to an understanding of the economics of the situation. The ownership of the land mainly determines which firms succeed and which fail.

The entrepreneur, whether a large company or a sole trader, offers the retailing service by providing the capital, the employees, the supply of goods, and their quality and price. This service is subject, of course, to supply and demand conditions. The landlord, in sharp contrast, does nothing but sits back and collects the rent, owing to his claim to own the land. If the landlord works to maintain or improve the site, he clearly needs to be rewarded for his labour and capital. It is the charge made for location that is the obstacle, for location remains regardless of who lays claim to the land. A surplus exists, i.e. the economic rent, which can only validly belong to the whole community as the legitimate trustee.

For the retailing industry, location embraces proximity to the market, availability of transport, parking space for customers, suitable neighbouring shops or facilities like banking, law and order and other public services, even such features as being on the sunny side of the street. Perhaps the cardinal aspect of good retailing location is simply being central in a shopping area, or perhaps also being on a street corner. Which of these advantages is contributed by the efforts of a landlord, whether an absentee or one who is also an entrepreneur?

Landlords in Britain are distinguished by having freeholds or long leases. Other people pay rent, but they do not. Yet the difficulties encountered by retailers, demonstrated most poignantly by the many high streets with empty or dilapidated premises, do not arise from paying rent as such. The problem for them is caused by the need to pay taxes on labour, sales and profits at the same time as paying rent to a landlord. Were the rent to replace these taxes under a fundamental tax shift, entrepreneurs who do not own freeholds or long leases would prosper alongside those who are at present also landlords. The latter, of course, would be subject to the same regime of public rent collection, and likewise relieved of other taxation.

As with other industries, the situation with retailing is rendered more complicated by leases. With a very short lease, the landlord/entrepreneur relationship is simple. The entrepreneur has to pay rent and/or a capital payment for the lease, whilst the landlord receives rent periodically or as an upfront payment for the lease. Rent paid corresponds more or less to the economic rent of the land, plus rent for the premises. When the lease is longer, the economic rent may be divided between landlord and tenant, unless there are frequent revisions of the terms. How it is divided depends on many conditions, like the state of the retail market, supply costs, changes in public services and everything else that affects the state of the retailing firm. If these conditions improve during the period of the lease, the retailer may benefit greatly from the rise in economic rent. Nowadays leases are usually subject to revision of the rent in favour of the landlord, since both inflation and economic growth are foreseen when the lease is agreed. Such is the power of landlords and their legal advisers; witness the number of retailers who close down when their lease expires. Were a land value tax in place it would fall naturally to the account of whoever was receiving rent for the land (not, of course, for the buildings).

The effect of internet sales and online competition eating into the retail market is borne by entrepreneurs, if the landlords do not reduce rents accordingly, whereas a land tax would be cut if rents fell, thus inducing landlords to absorb the reduction in sales, rather than imposing it upon the entrepreneur.

Recent falls in high street sales have reduced the capital value of high street properties, but market values have tended to ignore the falls in order to maintain capital values as investment assets. Essentially this is an attempt to shore up values for the landlords.

This underlying system of land law has evolved over centuries, and has determined the form of the retailing industry throughout Britain. Notably it explains the demise of the high street as it existed until about the mid-twentieth century. Where once stood family shops of grocers, bakers, butchers, clothiers, hardware merchants and other very varied small firms, we now find supermarkets, chain stores of grocers, bakers etc. selling products characterised principally by standardisation. High streets all tend to look the same, with the same household names appealing to customers already conditioned to their products by mass advertising. Only the occasional local council has the initiative to grant planning permission on the basis of independent style, quality, tradition and local opinion, rather than under the financial pressure – some of which may be corrupt – from the giant retailers. How many high streets now boast small couturiers, independent bookshops, master bakers and the like? If they have survived, they are probably round the corner in a side street.

This is not to ignore the advantages of larger firms. A chain of clothiers may offer cheaper, better value products. A supermarket with a car park may be the most efficient means of shopping for many people, especially those hard-pressed for time by today's style and pace of life. The point is not that smaller is better. It is simply that fair competition would enable the most suitable and desirable retailers to prosper. Competition is largely absent because every retailer trades under conditions determined by the system of landownership and the present incidence of taxation. The site that pays rent and taxes is too heavily burdened. The one that is free of rent has a gross advantage. The marginal site suffers under a tax regime that demands the same rates of tax on labour, sales and profits as is levied on the best sites. So the couturier, the bookshop, the master traders are squeezed between the anvil of rent and the hammer of taxation, whilst the landlord and the freehold entrepreneur are relieved of the former.

This oppressive situation leads to the concentration of ownership in the hands of retail chains. Firms with freeholds, and especially those with better sites, become financially strong. They accumulate profits (which are really rent) for re-investment, and they can borrow heavily from banks or shareholders. Whilst banks drag the carpet from under the feet of struggling marginal shops, they finance the well-endowed chain store with ample 'capital'. Favourable locations are gradually taken over by the successful chains. Every town and city has its Boots, W.H. Smiths, Marks and Spencers, Waterstones and all the retailers who adorn our commercial television screens.

Supermarkets are the most obvious form of this concentration of retail ownership caused by the private receipt of rent of land. The grocery market in particular has become dominated by an oligopoly of Tescos, Sainsburys, Asda, Marks & Spencer, Morrisons and Waitrose, who control a high proportion of the best sites. They appear to be very competitive, even to the extent of price wars. But rent is not eliminated by price competition; that merely operates to limit the genuine profits that reward good entrepreneurship. This is confirmed when a supermarket closes down. It usually sells the site to a new firm, perhaps in a different class of product, with the epithet 'goodwill' attached to the sale. This is really a code name for the site value, as it means principally the attraction of the location for shoppers generally.

A further proof of the tightness of the grocery oligopoly is evident in the difficulty experienced by new entrants to the market. The best sites are already occupied. Developments on new sites face oligopoly's favoured devices of brand advertising, cut-price competition and deliberate over-capacity. The new entrant cannot readily match such methods of ruthless short-run competition.

Supermarket oligopoly leads to further unfortunate consequences. Standardisation has already been mentioned. It is closely related to brand advertising, which attempts to disguise standard products by superficial labelling. New entrants are faced with competing against an apparently large list of competitors. Consumers become immured to products that are household names, from toothpaste to bottled water. (This is related, of course, to mass production of the original product.) The proliferation of heavy lorries transporting goods to supermarket outlets from giant warehouses has also been referred to above. External diseconomies, like traffic congestion and pollution, are not attributed to their real cause. The actual costs (and benefits) of this system cannot be measured, especially since the small independent grocer cannot compete and reveal any greater efficiency or value.

An argument for the benefit of supermarkets that has some justification is that shoppers can buy a wide range of products in one location, which invariably has a car park. (One might enquire whether a fair rent is paid for the car park in many cases.) But the concentration of products under one roof does not demand single private ownership of the site. Town markets on council owned land offer a similar concentration of products, with rent being for once collected by a public authority. One can imagine a 'supermarket' in which each product area – bakery, dairy products etc. – were run by separate retailers. The 'supermarket' owners could rent the area from the council, and be rewarded for their skill and effort in providing the service by payment for wages, return of capital (including the building), and normal profits as entrepreneurs.

A final example of the futility of leaving rent of land in the hands of retailers was given by a major multinational coffee chain. The company admitted, or indeed boasted, that they only sell coffee in order to retain control of the site and cover the running costs. Most of their 'profits' come from the continual rise in the value of their sites, which were carefully chosen inner city locations throughout the world. Providing shoppers with a hot drink was purely incidental to the real business of making money out of land. We have become a rent-seeking society; so much for the myth of a competitive entrepreneurial economy.

14
Agriculture

M OST BRITISH PEOPLE would respond to any mention of a 'land question' by assuming that it refers to agriculture, or perhaps to conservation or forestry. This attitude exemplifies the extraordinary general lack of awareness that we all live on land, build our houses on land, shop on land, and work on land. It demonstrates too a wide lack of comprehension that urban land values have become a crucial feature of our economy, and indeed a major aspect of its endemic problems. Agriculture itself, however, remains a prime area where fundamental doubts may be raised about the terms on which land is owned and tenanted.

A threefold structure of landlord, tenant producer and landless labourer pervades the whole economy, but is particularly prevalent in agriculture. Agricultural land is usually privately owned. The skilled and demanding work of farming is performed by tenant farmers; and the third role is that of agricultural employees, some also highly skilled, others working as farm labourers.

This threefold division is not always matched by a neat distinction between the actual role players. The landlord is sometimes a working farmer. Moreover, a landlord's provision of improvements to the land, such as drainage or fencing, amounts to a productive investment for which any net income received is not rent but wages or profits. On small farms the farmer himself may also labour on the land, and perhaps not have any employees. Nevertheless, as always in Economics, the functions need to be kept in mind, regardless of the persons involved.

What do these functions yield to the participants? In so far as he is an entrepreneur, organising the farm and taking the risks of the market – and the weather! – the farmer receives wages and profits. He pays rent to the landowner, or keeps it as rent if he is the owner. He pays wages to the employees. This triple division into rent, wages and profits is very often concealed under the heading of 'farm incomes', a confusion which also hides the basic fault in the whole structure of agriculture. For example, subsidies, whether paid by the European Union or by the British government, becomes a fudged issue.

One may ask whether all three functions in the farm industry are strictly necessary. Clearly the farmer's work and risk-taking are essential. (The risk, of course, can be minimised by insurance facilities.) Equally the employees simply receive a return for their effort and skill. But what does the landowner offer, *qua* claimant to the land, as distinct from any productive investment or work on his or her part? The answer is surely nothing, unless one sees the rent paid as a return for not withholding the land from use! (And for that, rather than a return, surely there should be a penalty if the land were withheld from use, which a tax on all land value would automatically enforce.) Once again it seems that any payment for the use of the land should go to the community which creates its value. Rent of agricultural land should be collected as public revenue, whether national or local or both.

Capital employed in farming, like all capital, requires a return that meets its costs. Modern farming is very capital intensive with much large scale machinery and equipment. Owing to the substantial extra costs of employing workers, such as PAYE, NI and administrative costs, there is a strong incentive to substitute capital for labour, an effect which operates in other industries equally. Nevertheless, whoever provides the capital, whether the farmer or the landowner, earns a fair reward for the service, which is quite distinct from rent.

At present farm capital may often be provided by the landowner because he has the security in the form of a charge on land, required by the banks. Were a tenant farmer relieved of taxation, he or she could afford his own capital. Only those who are also landlords can do this with ease under today's conditions. Working farmers would become the true custodians of the industry, rather than the landlords who too often are seen as forming the backbone of the agricultural industry.

A tax shift to land values would have a further profound outcome for farming. Natural features of the land, as well as its location near markets, for example, greatly affect the productivity of farms. Variation of soil may determine the type and value of the yield in both crop and livestock production. Drainage and topography play important roles. Climate may favour dairy farming, and so on. Highlands of Wales and Scotland are especially suited to sheep farming. Market gardening prefers proximity to urban areas. Access to transport influences agriculture everywhere.

All these distinctions are reflected in the economic rent of land. Farm land in East Anglia is considerably more expensive than that in Cornwall. Such ubiquitous differences have extreme consequences for the industry. Financial institutions find it worthwhile to become landlords in Suffolk, whilst small marginal farmers in mid-Wales abandon their holdings, particularly if their product prices fall. Farmers who own good land become rich, but not principally by farming.

The large price differentials for farmland have far-reaching effects under the current regime of unconditional private ownership. At present the better land is very expensive. This encourages owners to hold more land than they may need for farming, thus making the land in use even more expensive and relatively scarce.

High land prices make it hard for new farmers who have little or no financial capital to enter the industry. Lack of collateral security prevents them from looking to bank credit, so existing landowners have a stranglehold on the industry. Their heirs alone are in a strong position to maintain the family ownership, but this is small comfort to keen new entrants. The same conditions limit the ability of enterprising tenant farmers to become owners.

A further inequity related to high land price is the completely random way in which fortunes may be made out of agricultural land, sometimes even marginal in nature, which abruptly acquires a very high price from the grant of development rights. A decision by the local authority to give planning permission may transform a relatively poor piece of farmland into a valuable site for development into a housing estate or similar project. The owner receives a gratuitous sum many times the previous value of the land, not for any effort on his or her part, but merely by having unconditional rights over the land, acquired by inheritance or by previous purchase at a low price. The land may have been deliberately held out of use in the expectation of the grant of planning permission. Such a system is a roulette wheel, rather than natural justice. The same criticism may be made beyond the range of agricultural land.

Farmers on marginal land are key elements in the economy of the countryside. Their dilemma, in principle, is the same as that of marginal firms in all industries, notably in retailing. They cannot afford to pay rent and taxes. The double burden of these charges that do not directly help to raise the value of their output is too much to bear. Especially so is this for taxes on labour, like PAYE and NI. These make the cost of hiring labour excessive. To employ two men costs as much as it would to pay three men the same total amount free of taxes. Fuel taxes are also difficult for remote farms with high transport costs. Were taxes levied on rent the burden would be removed from farmers.

Labour taxes clearly also reduce the level of employment in the industry. This reinforces the detrimental effect mentioned earlier of excessive substitution of capital for labour. Without labour taxes, employers would employ both labour and capital in the most efficient ratio, taking account of their productivity on one hand and their cost on the other. For these two reasons, employment generally in the countryside is artificially reduced, and the drift towards urban concentration enhanced. Failure to maintain rural amenities and traditions is yet another consequence.

Low agricultural wages also tend to deter British workers and draw in migrants, which has created social problems in some areas.

In view of the referendum result to leave the European Union, the question of farm subsidies requires a fresh approach. If they continue to be paid by the UK government will the same irrational system remain in force? Who needs subsidies – farmers or landowners? Clearly they should be paid to farmers in exceptionally adverse circumstances of weather, flooding or a collapse of market prices, for example. Even here a good insurance system should minimise the need for public assistance. But should any subsidies at all be paid to landowners? Where land has been fortuitously damaged, the cost of repair may be a legitimate claim, on the assumption that the landowner has been responsible for its maintenance. Any further subsidies to landowners would be simply to recognise a claim over the land which has no rational basis.

Yet one may question whether even farmers themselves really need public support. Marginal farms would be fully self-supporting if they were relieved of the double burden of rent and taxes. As things stand they pay heavy taxes with one hand and receive subsidies with the other!

Environmentalists might object to a land tax on the grounds that it would force landowners to develop marginal land, thus destroying the countryside. But, on the contrary, it might lead them to abandon such land, so that 'rewilded' land would bear no tax.

Agriculture is perhaps the most obvious example of an industry distorted by a grossly misdirected tax system. Working tenant farmers pay twice over for the services they require from the community: public infrastructure for transport etc., proximity to labour and markets, waste collection, law and order, all these and more increase the rent that the landowner can charge the farmer, whilst at the same time the tenant pays taxes and perhaps council tax for the very same services. What nature provides in good soil and climate, giving the land its inherent value, also forms a major element in the rent that is paid to an owner who has not created it.

15

Foreign Trade and Investment

F OR MANY DECADES the UK has struggled with the problem of its balance of payments with the rest of the world. Despite changes between fixed and floating exchange rates, between membership and non-membership of the World Trade Association, the European Free Trade Association and the European Union, and despite an emphasis on traditional British free trade, the problem has never been eliminated. A deficit on payments always threatens, underlain by a weak trading balance, only compensated by a fairly permanent surplus from a somewhat bloated financial services sector, or by large so-called inward investment.

What would happen to the balance of payments if the economy were reformed as outlined above, in particular by a tax shift? A great number of beneficial effects would follow. First, and perhaps the most important, would be a rise in productivity per worker. UK productivity lags seriously behind that of many other industrial countries. In 2016 UK came last in this respect amongst the Group of Seven. Workers in the USA and much of Europe produce more per hour, or work shorter hours for similar outputs. Explanations are manifold, including for example the weakness of UK technological education and the length of time travelling to work. Such conditions may explain the relatively poor performance, but the primary cause of low productivity must surely be the lack of connection, even alienation, between workers and the nature of their work. The great majority are employees, many in faceless large companies with absentee owners and remote directors. Those in small, well-managed firms may be closer to identifying with what they produce, with a consequent interest and pride in the quality of the product.

Were workers, including of course managers, at all levels of skill and expertise to be the owners of the capital used in their firm, and with some say in the policy of the firm, their productivity would surely rise. Present day workers who are self-employed clearly demonstrate this. Both sole traders and members of partnerships are engaged in work of their own choosing, and earn rewards commensurate with their contribution. (Although in marginal firms there are severe limitations.)

Reformed firms would also have greater flexibility in responding to market conditions, especially where world markets are competitive and volatile. This would be particularly true at the margins of production, where freedom from taxation, and with land and credit readily available, firms would be strong enough to withstand rapid or adverse changes in the market. A fall in demand would not necessarily lead to closure, as the response could include a reduction in wages which would not impoverish the worker/owners.

Indeed the removal of labour and capital taxes generally would lead to a reduction in the UK level of costs of production, and therefore of export prices. There would also be a reduction of imports, as UK goods became cheaper at home. Both effects would improve the balance of trade. Less monopoly and oligopoly would further reduce costs and prices by removing the mark-up from such non-productive features of the economy.

Today the UK economy is often described as unbalanced, in so far as the services sector amounts to over 70% of GDP, whilst manufacturing has fallen to about 12%. This ratio is reflected in the balance of payments, where a large surplus in financial services supports a serious deficit on manufactured goods. But of what do these financial services consist? Only a minority is made up of services essential to industry, such as banking, insurance or shipping. The remainder often reward speculation in one form or another. Hedge funds far exceed in volume and complexity the extent to which they fulfil the genuine market requirement of ironing out excessive fluctuations in volume and price.

The foreign exchange market is perhaps the clearest example. Over 95% of daily transactions are for speculation, whilst the odd 5% fulfil the original function of providing foreign exchange needed by traders. Profits and commission on speculative deals is a dubious way for the UK to balance its books. A return to the days when the London financial market offered real services to UK and foreign businesses would be both an economic and moral benefit.

There can be no doubt that an economy in which there were high productivity, good quality products, no labour or capital taxes, unhampered bank credit, public monopoly only, flexibility to adapt to market conditions and a healthy balance between services and goods would be strongly based to support the principle of world free trade. This would be so even were it a unilateral policy facing protection abroad, for the UK would become an exemplary economy, soon to be followed by more progressive nations and organisations abroad, as it was in the late nineteenth century. Once more, the world would follow where the UK leads.

There remains the question of so-called foreign investment. Inward movements of financial capital, where domestic firms are bought wholly or partially by overseas 'investors', is universally hailed as a bonus for the economy. All British political parties seem to approve of it without reserve. More and more British industries are becoming dominated by foreign ownership. Yet what this process really represents is the failure of the UK banking system, whose proper function is to provide credit for home-based firms. At present, the credit they extend is largely for house purchases on mortgages and for investment by firms offering land as collateral security. Hence overseas banks and other institutions or companies move to fill the gap in credit for UK industrial production.

As a consequence of this unnecessary situation, foreign owners have the power to decide on the policy of many British firms, including whether to close down, to relocate abroad, to set conditions and pay for workers, and generally to determine the whole future of the firm. All this is far removed from a rational structure of industry, whereby those who actively participate in the work of a firm have control over it, either directly or through representatives. It is absentee ownership writ large.

The counterpart of this is UK investment abroad. Likewise one may ask why UK firms, including banks, should feel the need to send financial capital or give credit abroad, even to the extent of controlling foreign firms, when they should be providing these facilities for domestic production. In a truly reformed economy the attractions of investment at home would easily outweigh those abroad.

The correct meaning of investment is the construction of capital goods, or by extension of meaning the purchase of capital goods. Almost all overseas investment, both in and out of the UK, consists merely of movements of funds, with no real investment taking place. Moreover, land is not capital, so that the purchase of land is in no way a capital transaction, even though capital, such as a factory or office, may be bought at the same time. Were the price of land to fall, perhaps to zero, with rent being collected as public revenue, almost no such sham overseas investment would take place. Were only the UK to have such a fundamental reform, at least inward investment would be directed away from unproductive rent-seeking. British land would also remain British.

What of interest payments and the rate of interest? Under a reformed system of banking UK interest rates would merely be a charge for actual bank services, with a small premium for risk. Foreign banks would be unable to charge more than domestic ones, so they would keep probably to other opportunities to make high interest charges.

But would UK banks not be tempted to provide credit abroad where their return would be greater? The interest rate differential would seem to draw funds away from UK firms looking for cheap available credit at home. This could be a case for government intervention to withdraw banking licences from banks dealing excessively abroad, but a more liberal solution would be to allow the greater risk of default by foreign firms to provide a limit. Risk within the UK would undoubtedly be low in view of the new structure of industry, involving much higher wages that would finance capital investment. No longer would firms survive on narrow margins remaining when costs, rent and taxes have been paid. The interest rate differential between the UK and abroad would be viable.

Finally there is the exchange rate. For some time the trading account deficit has threatened to reduce the exchange rate for the pound, with financial services and inward investment preventing its collapse. This situation might go into reverse. A trade surplus would surely emerge, sufficient to nullify the effect of reduced financial services and a fall in 'imports of capital'. Hence the pound would strengthen, rising gradually as structural and credit reforms became effective. Certainly the UK economy would no longer be threatened by the need to adopt policies merely to hold up the exchange rate and prevent a balance of payments crisis.

16

Historical Outline

THE IDEA of raising public revenue from the rent of land may sound like a revolutionary one to many people, or at least a new and perhaps alien idea in defiance of well-established conventions, such as the prevalence of income and sales taxes. On the contrary, when examined historically the reverse is true. Taxes on the value of land have an ancient origin, and have only fairly recently been replaced by today's income based system.

Republican Rome treated land as the main source of public revenue, until this was gradually overtaken by the greed for land that culminated in the *latifundia* (great estates) that spelled the death of the Empire.

In Anglo-Saxon England food-rents payable in kind were assessed on hides of land, and the *trinoda necessitas* consisted of charges on land to finance the *fyrd* (army), fortresses and bridge building. Norman feudalism brought in a new system of charges on land, in the form of service in the royal army, or other types of service for a lord and indirectly to the king. When such service was finally commuted to money payments, a rudimentary system of land taxes had emerged.

In Tudor times serious land enclosure began, as common fields were taken, often for conversion to sheep farming by individual landowners. As R.H.Tawney wrote, when feudalism ended the poor law began, as peasant farmers lost their traditional rights in land. Men like Thomas More and Hugh Latimer protested against this unrestrained landownership, but by the seventeenth century enclosure had eaten up a great deal of the commons, to the extent that during the Civil War the cry went up 'whose slaves the poor shall be?' The True Levellers, led by Gerard Winstanley, tried in vain to limit the new kind of unconditional claims on land, which were to lead to the idea that land could be treated as an object of absolute private possession with no acknowledgment of public rights in it.

Such economic movements were in no way unique to England. In France, for example, Rousseau protested that private ownership of land lay at the root of social inequality, and later in the eighteenth century, when feudal estates still dominated landscape, the Physiocrats, including such notable figures as Quesnay and Turgot, taught that land should be the sole source of taxes, since land alone produced a surplus. Adam Smith, influenced by this school of thought, also regarded a tax on land as the most equitable form of public revenue, as he saw that it had no damaging impact on production and trade. David Ricardo made this principle clearer by explaining how differential qualities of land give rise to substantial differences in rent.

Nevertheless, land enclosure and the reduction of land taxes grew apace, until the Younger Pitt introduced income tax to pay for the war with Napoleonic France. The great landowners in the House of Lords favoured the change away from land taxes, so that by the twentieth century taxation was based almost entirely on income and sales.

Insight into the merits of taxing land had not been quite eliminated. The Liberal Party, led by Campbell-Bannerman, preserved the idea, which had been greatly publicised by the American economist Henry George. In the budget of 1909, instigated by Lloyd George and known as the 'People's Budget', a new land tax was proposed on a small scale. With support from Prime Minister Asquith and Winston Churchill, the budget was eventually passed, after the Parliament Act had reduced the power of the House of Lords to intervene on questions of finance. But implementation of the land tax clauses was cumbersome, so that they were not effective by the time the First World War broke out in 1914.

The war drastically broke the continuity of politics and thought. The active campaign for a land tax was almost forgotten in the aftermath, with so many more immediate problems to be dealt with. Lloyd George and Churchill, in particular, became preoccupied with other aims, and the idea of shifting taxation back on to the rent of land was eclipsed.

In the Labour Party a small group remained who remembered its significance. When the second Labour government was formed in 1931, the Chancellor of the Exchequer, Phillip Snowden, assisted by a life-long advocate of land tax, Andrew MacLaren, introduced a measure to tax land in the budget. But a financial crisis, caused by the flight of funds out of the UK, probably as a consequence of the earlier overvaluation of the pound when we had returned to the gold standard in 1925 and by a recession in 1929, led to the collapse of the government and the formation of a National government dominated by Conservatives. The land tax was repealed.

During and after the Second World War much land was acquired by the state for the MOD, forestry and nationalised industries. The imputed rent of this land contributed to such results as low rents for council house tenants. More recently the government has sold off much state land in order to fill gaps in the budget.

A few minority organisations have continued to recommend the replacement of existing taxes by the collection of rent. Today the Liberal Democrats retain it as an often overlooked item in their programme. Yet there are positive signs in the media and elsewhere that the symptoms of economic decline associated with the present tax structure will eventually lead open-minded people, including perhaps some economists and politicians, to appreciate the real importance of taxing rent as a surplus, rather than burdening productive enterprise.

There have been, of course, a few half-hearted attempts to recover unearned increment from appreciation of land values. These include taxing gains resulting from the grant of development rights, extending differentials on local rates, and increasing stamp duty on the sale of houses. Such piecemeal efforts reflect the lack of understanding of the universal presence of land rent in the economy. They have usually been repealed, when inflation and administrative difficulties have exposed their inadequacy.

Economic thought has reflected, or anticipated, the failure of actual economic reform. After the Physiocrats in France and Smith and Ricardo in Britain had expressed clearly the case for basing taxation on land values, economic theory took several steps in a contrary direction. Karl Marx and socialists influenced by him developed a theory of surplus value derived from the exploitation of workers that seemed – wrongly – to explain away rent of land as subsumed within this surplus value. The struggle between employers and workers was seen as a reflection of a fundamental opposition between capital and labour alone. The crucial third factor of land was largely ignored.

Whereas Marxist theory became a radical alternative to conventional Economics, the latter was itself seriously modified by the ideas of the American economist, John Bates Clark. Earlier economists had stressed the two major differences between land and capital, namely that the supply of land is fixed and that land varies greatly in type and quality. Clark argued that capital is also fixed in supply, ignoring the fact that this is only a short-term condition, as its supply responds to supply and demand in time. Secondly, Clark claimed that capital, like land, receives a return similar to rent, owing to differences in quality. This argument is also flawed in that the returns to capital are simply aspects of its supply price or cost of production, whereas the return to land is a pure surplus.

Clark's aggregation of land and capital seemed to conform to the contemporary condition of the American economy in the late nineteenth century. Entrepreneurs and speculators were making huge gains from rising land values in industries such as railways, mining and urban development, especially as the western States grew in population. They welcomed the apparent justification that they were simply providing much needed capital, rather than also receiving a surplus created by the rapid growth of the whole economy across the continent.

Economic theory has never corrected Clark's fundamental error. Few economists today acknowledge significant differences between land and capital. For example, the term 'investment' is used indiscriminatingly to refer to the purchase of both capital goods, like buildings and machinery, and land. 'Investment' in land does not create any new land; primarily it raises the price of land that has always in principle been available. Consequently, too, the rent of land habitually gets subsumed under profits in commercial accounts.

Clark was not alone in seriously confusing the whole basis of economic theory. Other economists, notably the leading British economist at the beginning of the twentieth century, Alfred Marshall, claimed that rent was merely the difference between the various use values of any asset, including land. For example, the difference between the income derived from using land for housing and using it for its next best use, such as manufacturing, is rent. This new concept of rent is not wrong. What is disastrously wrong is to equate this concept of rent with the Ricardian one. They are quite different with quite different implications.

The rent of land is calculated in principle with all sites of land in their best use. It is then the difference between the income derived from a particular site and the income from the same input of labour and capital at the most marginal site. The rent of the first site is a measure of this difference. An analogy is to treat marginal land as having a kind of sea-level value of zero and any non-marginal site as having a value equivalent to its height above sea-level. This means that the rent of all land in total is vastly greater than the values calculated on different use values alone. To confuse these two concepts of rent is to dispel any hope of a clear theoretical analysis of the economy. Combined with Clark's identification of land and capital, it makes much current theory into an impassable quagmire!

In the twentieth century the whole subject of Economics underwent a major change when John Maynard Keynes gave it a new dimension known as macro-economics. This has become a chief tool of government, which endeavours to control the national economy, especially through fiscal policies that manipulate levels of public expenditure and taxation. However, macro-economics has even less regard for land in the economy than did the micro-economic theories that preceded it. It is significant that Keynes' key work, *The General Theory of Employment, Interest and Money*, has only four brief references to land, none of which remotely examine the real role that land plays. This neglect is precisely demonstrated in a leading text-book, which claims that 'nothing significant is lost by ignoring land in the analysis of an industrialised economy.' (Lipsey and Chrystal, *Positive Economics* p634, 8th Edition, 1995.)

One final point drives home this vacuity on the part of modern economic theory. Macro-economics makes much of the concept of the national income. Governments use it to measure the success of their policies. Yet the figure for rent in the GDP is not the true economic rent of land, for it only includes actual money payments plus imputed rents where no money payments are made. It thus greatly understates the actual economic rent based on the excess of the annual value of land over the annual value of marginal land.

Moreover, when land changes hands for a capital sum, this is excluded from national income as a capital payment, even though it is really a premium paid up front for the use of land. In these and other ways rent is grossly understated in national income accounts. In fact, the whole system of macro-economics, upon which national income accounts depend, is fraught with errors arising from such misleading concepts as that of 'investment', which includes expenditure on both land and capital. But this is a matter that requires considerably more analysis of National Income Accounts than is provided here.

17
Economic Justice

THREE ASPECTS of the economy have been singled out as requiring fundamental reform: taxation, land tenure and banking. Once more it must be emphasised that all three are connected in a way that makes their contemporaneous reform essential. Indeed the required changes in taxation and land tenure can be understood as one basic reform.

If one accepts the fundamental principle that land is a gift of nature to the whole community, it follows that the rent of land belongs to that community, rather than to individuals. In which case, to collect the rent as public revenue is not strictly a matter of taxation at all. It would simply be a return to the community of what is created by its presence. Nevertheless, treating land as an asset to be privately owned, with its rent belonging to individual owners, is a deeply embedded attitude in modern Britain, so that any public collection of rent is likely to be regarded as a tax.

For this reason, and others referred to below, the introduction of a new attitude, more conducive to natural justice, needs to be approached with great circumspection. In particular, any tax assessed on land values to collect the rent must be accompanied above all by a reduction in existing taxes. Otherwise it would be seen as an additional tax that would seem to burden yet further the industry of the nation – even though it would only really be collecting a surplus retained by unproductive sources. Were a tax shift to take place, it might begin with removing those taxes that are directly imposed on production, particularly those on the employment of labour.

Great care would also be needed in retaining and strengthening the security of tenure of land. Public opinion might easily fail to see that collecting the rent of land in no way precludes preserving rights of tenancy. Indeed they can be strengthened by giving those who work by mind and limb more security against dismissal and eviction. Those who control the workplace would become increasingly those who productively occupy it. Both entrepreneurs and employees would have greater freedom from oppressive tenancy agreements and excessive rents. So too would house owners with heavy mortgages and tenants beset by grasping landlords.

Mortgages apparently present a problem to the proposed tax shift. Taxing land values brings down the price of land proportionately. When the rent is collected as revenue the capital value of the land declines. A freehold house owner finds that his land is worth less, perhaps leaving him or her with negative equity, since the mortgage remains the same. In fairness should not the mortgagee, i.e. the lender, pay a share of the tax equivalent to the proportion of the land value that is mortgaged? The house price would not diminish, and would remain the property of the occupier.

Transactions in land generally raise questions about the impact of a tax on land values. If a sale were completed shortly before such a tax were introduced, for example, the seller would avoid the tax whilst the buyer would find his new asset had fallen in price. In principle this is not strictly unfair, if one regards an absolute right to own land as morally wrong. In view of present-day attitudes, however, there does seem to be a need to mollify the aggrieved purchaser. Here again it is essential to introduce land tax gradually, so that the immediate impact on the price of land would be fairly insignificant. It could be likened to the impact of a rise in income tax, which immediately reduces the value of earnings or other income, which indeed are more certainly the property of the recipient than are land values. Moreover, when land is exchanged there is very often an asset attached to it, usually a building. The value of this asset would not attract the tax, so the purchaser would only lose out on the land value. Admittedly he has acquired an 'investment' that will slowly decline in value, but this is already a daily occurrence in asset markets of all kinds.

What would be the effect of a land tax on the inheritance of land? It would be a matter for society itself to decide the outcome. If inheritance remained as an unlimited right, the tax would simply become an annual charge to the new owner. Presumably the heir would inherit security of tenure, along with the right to receive rent. Only the latter would be increasingly limited by the annual tax. Yet this would greatly modify the long-run influence of inherited land on the social structure, making it fairer for all.

The issue of improvements to land has already been mentioned. In the lifetime of the improving owner they should not attract a land tax, since they are the outcome of work and capital. This could be implemented easily by allowing the owner to charge invoices for improvements against the tax assessment. For those, however, who benefit from the improvements, such as a legatee or purchaser, tax should be levied on the improvements as well as on the unimproved land. Almost all land in the UK has been improved at some time or another, so improved land must be the subject of a land value tax. This in no way would allow the assessment to be levied on buildings or other constructions attached to the land.

All these issues require careful discussion in a democratic society. Most of them might be settled fairly in several different ways. What is vital is that none of them should be used to obscure the fundamental principle that land value arises from the community and in justice should be returned to the community.

What then of banking measures, the third ingredient of our reform programme? Banks create money. At present they create it by advances to finance land purchase or investments in which land is a large element. Such advances are non-productive, since land is not produced, and therefore does not require an advance to cover its cost of production, as is the case with the production of capital goods. Advances for land purchase merely push up the price of land and reward landowners unnecessarily.

But in the present state of the economy land is not available for productive purposes, including housing, unless it is 'bought' in this way. Hence only the reform of taxation and land tenure as explained above would enable land prices to be reduced pro rata by a tax on annual land values. If land prices were seriously reduced, bank advances to buy land could be largely eliminated.

The beneficial result of this would be that banks could greatly increase their provision of credit for productive purposes. They would fulfil their true function of financing investment in the proper sense of providing industry with funds to finance production that takes time. In short they would offer credit where it is really needed.

Economics, like any subject that claims to be a science, is a search for natural law. Over the course of at least two centuries economists have indeed discovered its operation in many fields: supply and demand, diminishing returns, the use of money, international trade, exchange rates, market structure and many others. Yet, almost universally, they have failed to see the significance of one fundamental law, namely the law of rent. Despite the work of Smith and Ricardo, and more recently of the American economist, Henry George, the part played by land and rent has been largely ignored. The oversight, sometimes deliberate where vested interests have intervened, has been disastrous.

In terms of practical economic policies the heart of the problem lies in the question of the source of public revenue. In the UK, governments of all complexions, at least since the early nineteenth century, have founded their revenue policies upon the taxation of income and sales. They have not acknowledged that the natural source of public revenue is the rent of land. By the nature of economic production the net produce flows in two streams, towards labour on one hand, and towards land on the other, for the third factor of capital simply receives what is sufficient for its own production. Hence the natural return to the individual is wages, and the natural return to the community is rent. This law operates in every economy at all times, for nothing is produced without labour and land. This may be demonstrated even in the most highly automated modern factory. Everything used in production there is brought in from outside, except the labour being exerted on the land that is present. The buildings, machinery and equipment are themselves the products of other labour on land. It is only through a glass darkly that we see an economy dominated by capital, and through a yet darker glass that we see it in terms of money and financial capital.

Taxing labour and capital instead of land has a variety of detrimental effects. All firms are hit at their margin of production, so that they employ fewer workers than would be profitable without the taxation. In addition they tend to substitute capital for labour, if wages are especially heavily taxed. Both effects create a permanent pool of unemployed workers. The absence of free marginal land prevents the unemployed from working there. Were such land available there would be a new growth of business enterprise. This does not mean a resort to small-scale farming, but the formation of new firms and the creation of new entrepreneurs.

Alongside the neglect of the land factor has been a gross misunderstanding of the role of money and credit in the economy. Their natural function is to facilitate exchange, and to enable industry to employ labour and capital in advance of receiving the revenue from production. In short, credit is required because production takes time. Banks are the institutions that should fulfil this crucial function. Instead, today they are largely engaged in creating money by advances to buy land, especially for housing, and in limiting productive credit to firms that offer land as security.

Banking reform must follow upon land reform and taxation reform, since in present circumstances bankers have little option but to give credit against the security of land. To give credit primarily to productive industry requires that industry is founded upon security of land tenure without the burden of both rent and taxes. Once relieved of taxes on labour and capital, industrial enterprise of all kinds would be fully creditworthy. There would be a true level playing field, rather than the random pattern of insecurity offered by present conditions.

Reform is ultimately a moral issue. We all need to examine whether we are receiving from the economy the equivalent of what we offer to the economy by our effort and skill. By natural law, land is not to be offered by individuals in return for rent. The whole community may offer land for production in return for its rent to be used for public purposes, while banks may provide credit for production. Until these principles are widely accepted there will be no end to gross inequality, poverty and dispute. Once accepted, prosperity and social harmony may reign, for justice resides in the banishing of ignorance.

Indeed economic justice is the true end of both economic thought and of economic policy. Such ends as a high growth rate, full employment and a fair distribution of wealth and income arise naturally as fruits of justice. They would be achieved, not by making them prime targets, but by changing to conditions that bring them about. Civil justice has been established in Britain by the rule of law and eternal vigilance. May economic justice emulate it by study and application of the laws of natural justice in the field of economics.

Index

A NEW MODEL OF THE ECONOMY

BRIAN HODGKINSON

'... has serious implications for any economist or politician hoping to remedy ominous symptoms of disaster, like the current banking crisis ... In short, the book offers a model for fundamental reform'

Abstract of Public Administration, Development and Environment

This book is a radical revision of modern economic theory, but it deliberately follows the broad outline of modern textbooks. The aim is to revise some of the most basic concepts of economics to change the way we think about the economy. The effect would be a new attitude and new policy judgments towards the economy with practical and political implications.

The book is a response to the perceived need for a new economic model. It is not presented as a mathematical model, though diagrams are used, but rather as an amendment of the present framework of micro and macro economic analysis, changing the assumptions. These are related especially to (a) the fundamental part played by land, in its proper sense of all natural resources available on the earth, (b) the significance of credit, especially through the banking system, and (c) the crucial impact of the method and incidence of taxation.

The book draws upon the masters of economic thought from Smith and Ricardo to Marshall, Schumpeter and Keynes, by highlighting concepts often omitted from current studies of their works. This yields a thoroughly revised version of the contemporary model of a capitalist economy, revealing a genuine 'third way'.

'Presents a new model of economic theory that takes into consideration the idea of spatial location'

Journal of Economic Literature

ISBN 978 0 85683 279 6   £19.95 PBK

THE SCIENCE OF ECONOMICS
THE ECONOMIC TEACHING OF
LEON MACLAREN

RAYMOND MAKEWWELL Ed.

Leon MacLaren (1910-1994) was a barrister, politician, philosopher and the founder of the School of Economic Science. He considered the true goal of Economics to be the discovery of the conditions which allow every individual to find a fulfilling life. He defined economics as 'the study of the natural laws which govern the relationships between people in society'.

This book is based on a three-year course prepared by him for the School of Economic Science in London in the late 1960s. The editor, Raymond Makewell, presents the original subject matter revised with more recent examples and statistics from Australia, Canada, New Zealand, UK and USA.

Instead of making supply and demand the starting point, it begins with the simple observation that all material wealth is ultimately derived from land, and, where goods are exchanged, the first requirement is trust or a system of credit. From this starting point the major characteristics of the modern economy such as banking, companies or corporations, international trade, taxation and trade cycles are examined in terms of the conditions that govern how and why they evolved and how they operate today.

The framework in which the economy operates is examined in terms of how the system of land tenure and the concepts of property evolved in the English-speaking world, the role of government in economic affairs, and the degree of economic freedom. This reveals how the current economic situation denies people access to all that they need to work and produce wealth for themselves. Injustice is the inevitable result and poverty its inseparable companion.

ISBN 978 0 85683 291 8   £14.95 PBK